The Tantric View of Life

BY THE SAME AUTHOR

sGam-po-pa: The Jewel Ornament of Liberation
(Rider & Co 1959, paperback 1970, Shambala 1971)

The Life and Teaching of Naropa
(Oxford at Clarendon Press 1963, O.U.P. paperback 1971)

Treasures on the Tibetan Middle Way
(E. J. Brill 1969, Shambala 1971)

The Royal Song of Saraha
(University of Washington Press 1969)

Buddhist Philosophy in Theory and Practice
(Penguin Books 1972)

Distributed in the Commonwealth and Europe
by Routledge & Kegan Paul Ltd
London and Henley-on-Thames

Vajradhara (rDo-rje-'chang): Symbol of the Absolute in its polarity aspect
(*Author's collection*)

THE TANTRIC VIEW OF LIFE

By HERBERT V. GUENTHER

SHAMBALA THE CLEAR LIGHT SERIES
BERKELEY AND LONDON 1972

FIRST PUBLISHED IN 1972
BY SHAMBALA PUBLICATIONS INC
1409 FIFTH STREET
BERKELEY, CALIFORNIA 94710
AND BARN COTTAGE, STERT
DEVIZES, WILTSHIRE

MADE AND PRINTED IN GREAT BRITAIN
BY T. & A. CONSTABLE LTD
EDINBURGH

ISBN 0–87773–028–8
LIBRARY OF CONGRESS CATALOG 78–146511

This book is published in THE CLEAR LIGHT SERIES
dedicated to W. Y. Evans-Wentz
The series is under the joint editorship of
Samuel Bercholz and Michael Fagan

TO THE MEMORY OF
J. R. McCULLOUGH

Contents

List of Plates

Preface

THE word Tantrism has become an accepted term in the English language, but apart from this fact there is little evidence that any serious attempt has been made to clarify what this word implies and what that for which it stands means to the individual who becomes involved with the discipline of Tantrism. Generalizations about Tantrism are, as a rule, misleading because they rest on an insufficient factual basis. Before we can generalize we must know something of the underlying premises which have been guiding the development of Tantrism through the ages. In this book I have endeavoured to deal with these premises on the basis of indigenous Tibetan texts, rather than with individual Sanskrit works and their translations (although they, too, have been utilized) because the indigenous Tibetan texts go to the very root of Tantrism. The limitation of this approach is that I deal with Buddhist, not Hinduist, Tantrism; the advantage of this approach is that I avoid confusing ideas that have nothing to do with each other.

It is my conviction that Tantrism in its Buddhist form is of the utmost importance for the inner life of man and so for the future of mankind. If the life of the spirit is to be invigorated, there must be a new vision and understanding, and there is hardly anything of such value as the study of the experiences and the teaching of the Buddhist Tantrics. For Tantrism is founded on practice and on an intimate personal experience of reality, of which traditional religions and philosophies have given merely an emotional or intellectual description, and for Tantrism reality is the ever-present task of man to be.

The critical references to Western ideas, assumptions, and conclusions are not meant as a disparagement, but as a means to highlight the contrast between two divergent conceptual frameworks, the one, predominantly mechanical and theistically nomothetic; the other, basically dynamic and existentially appreciative. Unless these points of divergence are made clear only a mystificatory hotchpotch and a cheap sentimentalism result.

I am greatly indebted to the Government of India, Archaeological Survey, for making available photographs of relevant sculptures.

I am also deeply grateful to my colleague Keith Scott for valuable criticism, to James Valby and, above all, my wife for preparing the typescript and the index.

Being – The Quintessence of Tantra: An Outline

The concrete presence of Being is twofold:
Presence of body and of mind.
The presence of the body means that
It is knowable in a gradation of coarse,
Subtle, and very subtle, generally indivisible.
From the radiant light (comes) a great blankness,
From this both enactment and appreciation come in a plurality (of life-forms)
(Which in turn is) five awakenings,
Structure, motility, and *bodhicitta* (life's energy).

(The Ground)
The concrete presence of mind means
That it resides in the center of the body as E-VAṂ,
Being of the nature of enactment and appreciation.
This is the fundamental awareness present in the body,
It is the abolition of all fictions.

(The Way)
Free from the concepts of *maṇḍala* and *(gaṇa)cakra*, of Karmamudrā and Jñānamudrā,
Do not negate, do not suspend (the mental working), do not find fault,
Do not fix (the mind on something), do not evaluate, but just let be.

(The Goal)
As the seed, so the tree—
As the tree, so the fruit.
Looking at the whole world in this way—
This then is relativity.

From Āhapramāṃasamyak-nāma-ḍākinī-upadeśa

The Significance of Tantra

When in 1799 the word Tantra was introduced into the English language, it was used with reference to a certain kind of literature that in many ways has remained baffling to those who have tried to fit it into the general, highly idealized and therefore utterly misleading, picture of Indian philosophies, which were assumed to be of one piece. Since the word Tantra occurred in both Hinduist and Buddhist book titles, these writings were first lumped together and then dismissed as inadmissive of 'clear' statements. The alleged obscurantism of this literature, however, was but a reflection of the shocking parochialism of those who had access to it and who assumed that what was not of Western origin consisted merely of a welter of myths and poetry, religion and superstition, and hence was negligible and contemptible. Moreover, since this literature included topics which were excluded from the 'respectable' domain of 'philosophy', assumed to be a repository of deep, clear and high ideals with little bearing on the harsh realities of actual life except in so far as it concealed them, a curious ambivalence resulted. Either the literature was said to reflect a sad state of intellectual and moral degeneration, or it was believed to contain the keys to a world of power and sex, the two basic notions that haunt all those who are lacking in the one or the other and especially those lacking in both. Although the degeneration theory has been largely abandoned, the assumption that power and sex are the primary concern of Tantrism is still widespread, for it is easier, and possibly more lucrative, to perpetuate ignorance than to gain and disseminate knowledge. The fact that in the Western world the word Tantra is almost exclusively used with reference to a power- and sex-inflated esoteric teaching and not at all in its broader connotation of 'expanded treatise', is highly illuminating as far as Western thinking is concerned, but it does not throw any light on what Tantra means in itself.

The word Tantra is used differently, and hence does mean different things to Hindus and Buddhists. This is also borne out by the underlying metaphysics so that Buddhist and Hinduist Tantrism are quite distinct from each other, and any similarities are purely accidental, not at all essential. Hinduist Tantrism, due to its association with the Sāṃkhya system, reflects a psychology of subjectivistic dominance, but tempers it by infusing the human with the divine and vice versa; Buddhist Tantrism aims at developing man's cognitive capacities so that he may *be*, here and now, and may enact the harmony of sensuousness and spirituality. Dominance or power has a strong appeal to the ego, as it enables the ego to think that it is the master of its world. Dominance also strikes a resonant chord in us who live in a mass society that threatens to annihilate the individual. Again it is power that seems to compensate for the inner feeling of despair. But unaware of the fact that the acceptance of power as the supreme value is the surrender of one's true individuality, a person who feels insecure and is afraid of becoming himself may turn to anything that seems to promise him the attainment of power. Because of this slanted view and because the word *śakti* 'creative energy', frequently used in Hinduist Tantra, but never in Buddhist Tantra, could be understood as 'power', the word Tantrism has almost exclusively become synonymous with Hinduist 'Tantra', and more is known about it than about Buddhist 'Tantra' which stresses individual growth and tries to realize the uniqueness of being human.

In Buddhism, Tantra means both 'integration' and 'continuity', as is stated in the *Guhyasamājatantra*:[1]

> " 'Tantra' is continuity, and this is threefold:
> Ground, Actuality, and Inalienableness."

Tantrism begins with the concrete human situation of man's lived existence, and it tries to clarify the values that are already implicit in it. Its gaze is not primarily directed towards an external system which is passively received by observation and then dealt with as an object of some kind; nor does Tantrism speculate about a transcendental subject beyond the finite person. Rather it attempts to study the finite existence of man as lived from within, without succumbing to another kind of subjectivism. Man's existence as it is lived in the concrete is quite distinct from the limited horizons of more 'objective' reason and science which have their distinct values but are not the only values; and it is known in a different way. The world of man is not some solipsism (subjectivism at its peak) nor is it the sum total of all the objects that can be found in the world; the world of man is his horizon of meaning without which there can neither be a world nor an understanding of it so that man can live. This horizon of meaning is not something fixed once and for ever, but it expands as man grows, and growth is the actuality of man's lived existence. Meanings do not constitute another world, but provide another dimension to the one world which is the locus of our actions. In this way, Being is not some mysterious entity, it is the very beginning and the very way of acting and the very goal. It is both the antecedents of our ideas and what we do with them for the enrichment of our lives. The emphasis Buddhism places on knowledge (*ye-shes*, *jñāna*) and on discriminative-appreciative awareness (*shes-rab*, *prajñā*) is the outcome of the realization that the human problem is one of knowledge and that knowledge is not merely a record of the past but a reshaping of the present directed towards fulfilments in the emerging future. This, then, is the meaning of Tantra as 'continuity'. Its triple aspect, as outlined in the aphorism from the *Guhyasamājatantra*, is explained by Padma dkar-po as follows:

> "The actuality or actual presence of all that is, ranging from colour-form to the intrinsic awareness of all observable qualities, is called 'concrete existential presence'. Since this is unalterably present, like the sky, (in everything) beginning with sentient beings and ending with Buddhas, it is termed 'Tantra as actuality' because of its continuousness.[2]
>
> "It is a way because it has to be travelled by (means of our) actions which mature and become pure in this unsullied Being, and it is a gradation because it continuously

proceeds from the level of the accumulation of knowledge and merits to the level of a Sceptre-holder. Hence it is called a 'gradation of the way'.[3]

"Since it is the ground from which all virtues grow and in which they stay, it is called 'Tantra as ground', and it is called 'Tantra as action' because it is the concomitant condition for becoming enlightened.[4]

"Goal is the attainment of the state of a Sceptre-holder who is the source of 'being-for-others', characterized by being free from incidental blemishes, and since (the process of) becoming enlightened continues as long as there are sentient beings as inexhaustible as the sky, there is gradual emergence (of fulfilment) and this gradual emergence of the goal is called 'Tantra as Goal'. Since this is characterized as an overturning of the obstacles set up by experientially initiated potentialities of experience, and as not incurring the loss of 'being-for-others' as in the case with a Nirvāṇa, in which awareness ceases, it is 'Tantra as Inalienableness'."[5]

There is thus no escape from Being, and what Tantra is telling us is that we have to face up to Being; to find meaning in life is to become Buddha—'enlightened', but what this meaning is cannot be said without falsifying it. Therefore, also, the knowledge on which Tantrism insists is not knowledge of this or that, of nature, society, or of the self, but the knowledge that makes all these kinds of knowledge possible. Similarly, the action it advocates is not an action which fits a person effectively into the context of a preconceived scheme but an action which is self-disciplinary and responsible. Responsibility is not merely action, rather it is a view of the one real world from another perspective, which as the goal is the realization of what we have been all along, because it is no less Being than the ground or starting-point. The passage from the hidden presence of the existential values to their existence is openly recognized.

It is in tune with the practical nature of Tantrism that it is centred on man, though not in the sense that 'man is everything', which is to depersonalize and to depreciate him as much as to subordinate him to a transcendental deity. The problem is not man's essence or nature, but what man can make of his life in this world so as to realize the supreme values that life affords. If there is any principle that dominates Tantric thought, it is so thoroughly a reality principle that nothing of subjectivism in contrast to an 'objective' reality remains. In the pursuit of Being there is a joyousness and directness which appears elsewhere to be found only in Zen, that is, the culmination of Sino-Japanese Buddhism, not the dilettantism of the retarded adolescents of the West, which in certain quarters at least is already on the way out. By way of comparison, Tantrism can be said to be the culmination of Indo-Tibetan Buddhism.

The Body as On-going Embodiment

TANTRA, divested of its mystifying accretions, has been shown to signify what we, for want of a better term, refer to by the word 'Being' or 'Existence', and its concrete presence is manifested in what we are accustomed to call body and mind. So we read in the *Āhapramāṇa-samyak-nāma-ḍākinī-upadeśa*:[6]

> "The concrete presence (of Being) is twofold:
> Presence of body and of mind."

It seems as if Tantrism here merely repeats our own customary dualism and implicitly restates our evaluation of these two aspects of our existence. In order to dispel any misconceptions about Tantric intentions due to a seemingly similar wording and presentation, it may be worth while to survey the development of our dualistic approach and its innate evaluative character. Starting from Orphic-Dionysiac ideas, Plato removed first the soul out of the material world and changed the latter from being a divine whole to a realm of evil. This concept of two antagonistic and irreconcilable opposites proved itself so influential over the centuries that until recent times the dualism of body and soul was considered as being almost self-evident. It was only natural that on the basis of such reasoning the body should lose its value completely and even become an object of aversion. "The body is a tomb" (*soma sema*) says Plato in his *Gorgias*, taking up an expression that had previously been used by Philolaus. However, the condemnation of the body and its accompanying devaluation does not ensure the spirituality and undisputed value of the soul, since the soul contains ideas and thoughts, impulses and desires, of a material kind. Therefore the soul, too, had to be purged of the corporeality residing in it. Again it was Plato who depreciated not only the body but also the soul which, although participating in the higher realms of Ideas, pertains to the lower world of becoming. Superior to the soul was the spirit, a completely immaterial power. In this gradation, spirituality becomes synonymous with hostility towards the world and contempt for all mundane ties. Two contrary conclusions were drawn and both had (and still have) their respective representatives: the ascetic and the libertine. Asceticism is animated and sustained by fear. It grows on a strict dualism and takes the danger of contamination of what the ascetic believes to be the 'best' in man, his eternal element or whatever else he may call it, very seriously, and it attempts to render the contaminating power harmless, to oppose its operations, even to torture it, so that the soul or spirit may free itself and reign supreme. Asceticism is thus a search for power and pleasure by inverted means (deriving pleasure from torture). Although not all ascetics are psychopaths and lustful perverts, many have been and now still shine in the galaxy of saints.

The alternative to asceticism is libertinism. But unlike asceticism it is not based on fear, but on contempt. The utmost contempt for the body and for the world as a whole consists in dismissing it even as a danger. The body, and matter in general, is not only evil but *so* evil that the best thing to do is to raise oneself miles above it and in reckless bravado to do what one likes with it. Although libertinism often appears as a revolt against asceticism, both are of the same root. The one repudiates the body by non-use, abstention, the other by indulgence, overuse. Both are alike in their indiscriminate negativism. In the course of history, asceticism has usually been favourably commented upon, simply because its negativism lends itself admirably to institutionalization. Its depreciation of natural values may conceive itself as productive of a positive quality—purity, although in the ascetic framework it is essentially a rejection and merely develops a code of negative 'virtues'. On the other hand, libertinism has always remained the privilege and the prerogative of the 'elect', the pneumatics (spiritual ones) as contrasted with the psychicals and hylics. From this negativism inherent in asceticism and libertinism it is only a small step to utter nihilism—modern Western man's predicament. In terms of asceticism this means, 'destroy in order to save' (what or whom?), in terms of libertinism, 'hand in the body-count'.

The devaluation of the body and the rejection of the world as exemplified by asceticism and libertinism, reaches its climax in the idea of transcendence. Conceived as something other, yet not standing in any positive relation to the sensible world, it is the negation and cancellation not only of the world but also of itself. This nihilism is not countered by a so-called transcendental meditation, which is merely a restatement of the nihilism in non-Western terms. What is really transcendent is beyond being, and not a cause that gives certain properties of itself to its effect. It does not help us to understand ourselves or our world, but it apparently makes nihilism and nothingness palatable.

The depreciation of the natural world and of natural values accounts for the fact that little attention has been paid to the body, although without our body we would be nowhere, and, on the basis of such depreciation, the significance of the body cannot be understood. Nor is this possible by returning to a 'cult of the body' as it was practised in the pre-Christian world, particularly in Greece, where the passionate scrutiny of the naked body was subordinated to the intellectual interest in geometry and dealt with by way of 'proportion', which ultimately contributed to the rejection of the body as lived by a person. Nor is it possible by the allegedly therapeutic body groping, as this is merely the bestowal of an aura of respectability on what people all over the world have been doing all the time mostly and mainly clandestinely.

Body and mind, which for us are a set of opposites with mind having a 'higher' value, are in Tantrism interdependent and interpenetrating; the encompassing is also the encompassed. This is beautifully illustrated in the *Hevajratantra*:[7]

> "How could there be bliss if the body were a non-entity?
> It would be impossible to speak of bliss.
> Bliss encompasses (pervades) the sentient beings,
> In a manner of the encompassing being the encompassed.

As the fragrance of a flower
Could not be known without the flower,
So bliss would be a non-entity
If form and the like were non-entities."

The body is of primary importance, and this is indicated by the fact that the text speaks of its 'concrete presence'. This presence is an availability, a potency, which involves a kind of knowledge that differs from any intellectual or other construction which may be set up by way of scientific or other hypothesizing activity regarding the body. Thus the body is not some thing that man has, but man *is* his body. This has many implications. Therefore the *Āhapramāṇa-samyak-nāma-ḍākinī-upadeśa* continues:[8]

"The presence of the body means that
It is knowable in a gradation of coarse,
Subtle, and very subtle, generally indivisible."

With the exception of the phrase 'generally indivisible', which has found different explanations, there is agreement that the triple gradation refers to what is ordinarily meant when we talk about body, speech, and mind. The 'coarse', is both a 'collocation', or 'assemblage', and a 'continuum'. As a collocation or assemblage it comprises the five psychophysical constituents, i.e., colour-form as the epistemological object in a perceptual situation, feeling-judgment, sensation and concept-formation, motivation, and abstractive, categorical perception; the four elementary forces, i.e., solidity, cohesion, temperature, and motility; the six interactional fields, i.e., of the senses with their objects and of the mind with its ideas; the five sense-objects, i.e., colour, sound, fragrance, flavour, and texture; as well as the major and minor limbs. It is these which we would consider as making up the body as a 'thing' among other things. The other constituents we would consider as functions. The 'continuum' is set up by the encounter of the senses with their respective objects, sustained by appreciative discrimination, perspective, (subjective) disposition, unknowing, latent tendencies, desire, and the many emotions. This latter definition points to the individual's life-world with the body as an orientation centre with respect to which other objects are organized, cognized and valued in the spatio-temporal surrounding world. The life-world, the world of lived existence, is, as can be seen from the above definitions, neither wholly subjective (a mind) nor wholly objective (a body-'thing'), but both together in one. In this connection it is perfectly legitimate to speak of a 'human world' in which the body plays a very significant role; it does so because it is an animate organism, a complex (self-) structuring system in action.

The 'subtle' is the whole system of communication by means of linguistic patterns. It is midway between the 'coarse' and the 'very subtle' as it may be both a pattern, as for instance the sequence of the letters d-o-g, and a meaning as when I utter the word 'dog' to draw someone's attention to something.

The 'very subtle' is the unity of 'three manifestations', i.e., a dimming of the radiant light, a diffused glow, and a settled gloom,[9] which as concepts or 'constructs of the mind', 'emotions', and 'actions', set up what is known as Saṃsāra, the world, not so much in the sense of a container but as a movement from one situation to another, each demanding a solution which itself is most often just another situation. These 'three manifestations' do not act on the body from outside; they are, as the technical term indicates, its 'very subtle' aspect. As Padma dkar-po points out:

> "Its (operation) is not like that of a potter having made a jug which then continues without the potter, but like that of clay turning into a jug."[10]

On this view the body is a certain ensemble of 'potencies' and through it the body becomes the primal condition for the existence of the world. Not only do 'actions' issue from the body, but also the things perceived are orientated to this centre which thus is a kind of 'synergetic' system by which data of the most diverse kinds become unified and intended as pertaining to one identical state: I see a red rose, smell it, touch it, like it—the 'it' being intended as one and the same object by means of one and the same centre, the body. When in this context I speak of an 'I' doing all the above actions, this 'I' is not some entity added to the on-going process of singling out which permits me to speak of 'my body' by means of which there is 'my world'. Thus my body is indeed unique among all other bodies. *My* body is the only one in which I experience in an absolutely immediate manner the self-embodiment of *my* psychic life, i.e., a sensing, feeling, categorizing, and so forth. The body is thus present (and uninterruptedly presents itself) as the bearer (*rten*) of this or that psyche or life-force (*brten-pa*), and as an exterior presence which has within it the interior force (the psyche) which 'expresses' itself therein. This does not imply a hypostatization of the psyche (mind) as is done by the speculative idealistic-mentalistic philosophies. Tantrism is concerned with Existence which, in order to be meaningful as this or that kind of individual existence, must participate in absolute Being or Being-as-such, for which the Tantric texts use different terms; one that is most generally used is 'radiant light'. The presence of the body which, as the above analysis has shown, is a continuously on-going self-embodiment and self-expressiveness of psychic life by one body singled out as peculiarly 'its' own and felt and understood as 'my' body, is therefore 'indivisible' from this Being, the 'radiant light'. 'Radiant light' (*'od-gsal*) is a term for the excitatory nature of a living organism, by which is meant the capacity to increase or decrease its level of lumination. It does not imply a change from inertness to responsiveness. We, too, speak of a person glowing with joy, shining with happiness, radiating well-being. The luminousness of Being is the absence of all obscurity and its radiancy is its power to illumine, rather than a quality ascribed to it. The 'radiant light' belongs to us in our Being, but it diminishes in direct proportion to our being as circumscribed by categorical thinking. To the extent that we are 'lit up' we are happy and feel transported, blissful; but to the extent that 'the light goes out', we feel bored and depressed. sGam-po-pa has clearly stated this intimate relationship between 'radiancy' and 'bliss':

> "Radiancy is of two kinds, a cognitive radiant light and a radiant light that just is. The cognitive radiant light is not like the noetic principle, self-validating, self-luminous and absolutely real as claimed by the mentalists, but rather like a flame in a pitcher. The radiant light that just is, shines independently of another illuminating agent. The

> radiant light that just is, is, furthermore, happiness, but it is not an ordinary happiness that breaks, but absolute bliss."[11]

Since existence, Being-as-such, is an absolute value, my body, in so far as it shares in existence, is a value in its own right, regardless of the speculative ideas I may have about it as being this or that kind of object. Even on the basis of the traditional negative attitude towards the body, the claimant will cherish his body and is usually unwilling to part with it. This reveals a split we entertain between insight and opinion. Insight is concerned with Being, it sees what really *is*; opinion merely clings to what seemingly is, and loses itself in judging appearances. Opinion can never appreciate what is. Insight thrives on truth and understands it as absolute; opinion, too, clamours for truth, but replacing it by its own fictions, it is tied to dogmas which it tries to force on others because it is uncertain of itself and attempts to conceal this uncertainty by aggressiveness. To be is to let one's life be guided by insight, not by opinion. Applied to the body problem this means that insofar as I am my body which is the self-embodiment and self-expression of my psychic life, to the extent that my psychic life is guided by insight I really am, to the extent that it is (mis)guided by opinion I conceive of myself as *having* a body (which is despicable, or, in a milder form, more or less negligible) and a soul (that is to be saved). In a broader context the human situation turns out to be a quest, an emergency; man is a being who, in his being, is in search of his Being. Thus his Being is not only precious (*rin-po-che*) but also the very mystery (*gsang-ba*) of life as a problem involving man for whom it is a problem. It is so for me as an embodied being and so the *Vima snying-tig* speaks of four aspects of the body:[12]

> "The body is fourfold: (*a*) the body as a jewel and a mystery: this is Dharmakāya, Sambhogakāya and Nirmāṇakāya together.[13] (*b*) the body as pure awareness and apparitionalness: this is Sambhogakāya. Or, if the body as a jewel is Dharmakāya, this one is Rūpakāya. (*c*) the body as a conceptual system and tendencies: this is the sentient beings. (*d*) the body as mere cognitive possibility:

this is the state of suspension of mental activities and one at the level of formlessness."[14]

Once it is realized that the human situation is a quest based on the question whether insight and true being is realizable, the answer that this is possible is already anticipated, and the concomitant question, of how this situation in which I find myself has come about, is asked. The *Āhapramāṇa-samyak-nāma-ḍākinī-upadeśa* declares:[15]

"From the radiant light (comes) a great blankness,
From this both enactment and appreciation come in a plurality (of life-forms)
(Which in turn is) five awakenings,
Structure, motility, and *bodhicitta*."

The first point to note is that the human individual, in his quest, knows himself to be the subject of his quest, and this initial and original knowledge is the pre-supposition for the way he is going to judge himself in experiencing himself as the subject of his actions. The fact that the subject judges himself is not identical with the fact that the subject *is*, or *knows* himself *to be*. Judgment is not knowledge. It is made possible by knowledge, but it also is the nature of judgment that it replaces knowledge by its constructs. While in knowledge the subject 'knows', but does not judge, in judgment the possibility of meaningful life in and through knowledge is present as a challenge which makes any judgment dubious. Usually, this possibility of meaningful life is ignored, and true subjectivity is perverted into a self-defeating subjectivism, of which so-called 'objectivity' is its worst manifestation. It is on this distinction between Being-as-such, being knowing-subject, and the process of self-judgment, or subjectivism, that Tantrism bases its view of life.

Absolute Being, Being-as-such, present in the human situation as true subjectivity, is given many designations in Tantric texts; 'radiant light', 'great bliss', 'Mahāmudrā', and 'Tathāgatagarbha' are the most common ones. It is the nature of subjectivity to function, which means that the subject 'thinks' of its object as this or that, and in so doing soon 'judges' its object. This functioning-as-such is termed 'a great blankness' which is more specifically circumscribed by *ma-rig-pa* (*avidyā*). This is not so much ignorance, but a departure from and modification of the original knowledge through its functioning. It is still a blankness because the judgments have not yet been formulated, although they are there as possibilities. This blankness is, to use a simile, like the clear sky, in which at any moment clouds may appear. It should be noted that this blankness has nothing in common with the Lockean idea of a mental substance which is capable of consciousness when material substances affect it. Locke's idea fails to take into account the spontaneity and creativity of the living process, paramount in Buddhist thought, and attempts to reduce the nature of mind to mere passivity and receptivity.[16]

The possibility of appearance is termed 'enactment' (*thabs*) which then can be appreciated (*shes-rab*) and in this way lay the foundation of the various forms of life. More precisely, 'enactment' refers to the principle of action required in dealing with the world around us, including persons. The course of action required is specific for each living species, and in the realm of human beings it entails responsibility. But responsibility is something that most people are reluctant to assume. The recognition of the fact that life, existence, not non-existence, death, is the ultimate standard of value, determining the course of action, is also its 'appreciation' (*shes-rab*) and realization, because it is the capacity to discriminate between facts and fictions.

The plurality of the various forms of life is still halfway (*bar-do*) between pure possibility and an embodied state. However, the trend to become embodied in this or that particular existence continues to assert itself in the 'five awakenings' which result in our having and being our body. Therefore, when Tantrism speaks about the body, it actually speaks about embodiment which implies a certain structure, an on-going process or motility as the vehicle of psychic life. At the same time, embodiment in a particular form is a spiritual impoverishment in the sense that true subjectivity succumbs to the common subjectivism of ordinary existence. The term 'awakening' is purposefully ambiguous. We can awaken to our true Being and we can wake up to find ourselves in a situation which demands a solution. In awakening to

Buddhahood each of the 'five awakenings' corresponds to one of the five original awarenesses, but in awakening to a situation the absolute knowledge of subjectivity is lost sight of and so there are only four.

We have seen that the body as conceived in Tantrism is a complex of several strata. In one of them the body represents an orientational point as the centre of a particular ('my') milieu which, structured in terms of its own intentions, is actualized by means of its bodily activities, all of which are organized and oriented around the centre.[17] Another point to note is that the body is a sense-organ in the sense that my sensations are not mere 'sense-data', but components within a specific context of bodily activity.[18] The body thus is the bearer of localized fields of sensations (*āyatana*), (they appear [*skye*] *if* the organism is, for instance, touched and they appear or spread [*mched*] over the area *where* they are). Further, the body is itself co-experienced or co-intended simultaneously with the co-perception of the body as the means by which I perceive and as that by means of which what is perceived is perceived. This is technically known as 'togetherness' (*sahaja*), which applies to all strata.

While the body is the most immediate actualization of the on-going process of embodiment, that which embodies itself is termed *bodhicitta*, which literally translated means 'enlightenment-mind', but connotates what we would call 'life-force' or 'energy' operating through our 'body' or 'matter'. In order to prevent any misunderstanding it should be mentioned at this point that *no* relationship between a 'mind' and its 'body' is involved; rather, subjectively lived experiences as such are indicated. These experiences are viewed in terms of the indivisibility of the intentive processes (the intending and the intended). The intending as such is known as *karuṇā* 'compassion' and the intended as *śūnyatā* 'openness', or *vaṃ* and *e* respectively. This explains the often repeated statement that *bodhicitta* is the indivisibility of *śūnyatā* and *karuṇā*. Or it may be viewed as 'creativity' for which the most obvious symbols are 'semen' (*khu-ba*) and 'blood' (*rdul*), indicative of maleness and femaleness, and since creativity is a functioning, and since functioning means not to be at rest, to vary continuously, any one pole in this male-female polarity may be in the ascendancy. This, with reference to the body, means that sexuality is itself a mode of being of the person in question. In terms of the old body-mind division this would indicate that sexuality is as much physical as it is mental and, what is more, it is at once an object for others and a subject for me. Again, masculinity and feminity are indivisible, when the one is dominant the other is recessive and vice versa.[19] Lastly, as lived experience the *bodhicitta* is all-pervasive; it is, so to speak, both myself and my milieu.

This *bodhicitta*, which embodies itself and expresses itself in the body, is commonly referred to by the term 'mind' (*sems*), which is not so much 'consciousness' in our sense of the word, with distinct contents, but an 'original pristine awareness' in action. The *Āhapramāṇa-samyak-nāma-ḍākinī-upadeśa* says:[20]

"The concrete presence of mind means
That it resides in the centre of the body as E-VAṂ,
Being of the nature of enactment and appreciation."

Here again it is pointed out that the body is the centre of my actions and this centre has as its centre the *bodhicitta*; in other words, the *bodhicitta* or 'mind' is fundamental. In the symbolism of EVAṂ another very significant point has been noted. The vowel *E* is according to the Sanskrit language indicative of the locative case and an inflection of the vowel *A* which, as the first letter of the alphabet, stands for original *śūnyatā* (openness) which by virtue of its association with *prajñā* 'aesthetic appreciation' we can correctly understand as the open dimension of the perceptive field. Within it, that is, strictly within, as indicated by the locative case *E*, perception can move from one aspect of perfection to another and there are no limits to the richness of the perceptive field. The *prajñā* therefore roams over the whole of *śūnyatā* and it can do so because it is not tainted by any bias which obstructs intrinsic perception and aesthetic appreciation. This 'cognitive' process is supported by a continuous delight, symbolized by *VAṂ*. This continuous delight is an inalienable component of aesthetic perception and therefore the symbol *EVAṂ* is used. Each component seems to make the other more possible; the more a person is able to appreciate what there is, the more he feels contented, and the more contented he feels, the more he will be able to appreciate. There is in such an experience both depth and brightness, which contrasts sharply with the ordinary shallowness and dullness of our perception. But although we may speak of depth and brightness in aesthetic perception and aesthetic experience, they are not two, but inseparably together, and this togetherness (*sahaja*, *yuganaddha*) is the fundamental 'original and pristine awareness' (*ye-shes*) which we lose when we perform abstracting acts by attending to parts of things, by seeing the object not so much *per se* but as an instance in a larger category, in brief, by conceptualizing and indulging in the fictions of our own making about what there is. The *Āhapramāṇa-samyak-nāma-ḍākinī-upadeśa* continues:[21]

> "This is the fundamental awareness present in the body,
> It is the abolition of all fictions."

The above analysis of the body-mind problem in Buddhist Tantrism has shown that the body is the embodiment and thereby also the expression of an awareness whose body it is. Hence, all my bodily activities are experienced by me simultaneously as corporeal and subjectively lived. The awareness which embodies itself in and animates my body is thus fundamental. It is essentially an existential awareness in the sense that to be is to be aware. sGam-po-pa makes the following statement which literally translated would run:[22]

> "(With) Mind-as-such (*sems-nyid*) together (*lhan-cig-skyes-pa*)
> value-being (*chos-kyi sku*)—
> "(With) Appearance (*snang-ba*) together (*lhan-cig-skyes-pa*)
> value-being's light (*chos-sku'i 'od*)."

In our own diction it would say:

> "Mind-as-such is coterminous with Being-as-such as value,
> Appearance is coterminous with the light of Being-as-such as value,"

and in this coterminousness lies the spontaneity of life.

Appearance (*snang-ba*), which is another key-term in Tantrism, is not an appearance of something other than itself, a pitiable reflection as in Plato's thought, but the way in which an identical thing appears in its variations which are functionally correlated to the centre of the perceptive field. The light of the sun is not different from the sun, but is the sun as it appears to the beholder.

Buddhist existential awareness must not be confused with the subjectivism of modern existentialist philosophies. It is, to use the terminology of Abraham H. Maslow,[23] both a peak and plateau experience which carries its own intrinsic value with it and is *not in need* of a value-assignment. Existential awareness means that the mind, as a potential for this or that kind of experience, is directed towards values which through it become embodied, while in ordinary perception categories are the dominant feature. It is here that the split between subject and object occurs because 'subject' is as much a category word with certain presuppositions as is 'object'. The point is that both kinds of being or becoming aware are rooted in Being-as-such which is synonymous with Awareness or Mind-as-such, and man's problematic situation is that he can be his Being or his fictions. In whichever direction he moves, his problem will always be one of embodiment, which at the same time constitutes man's life-world.

The process of embodiment itself is illustrated by Karma Phrin-las-pa, commenting on Rang-byung rdo-rje's cryptic statement:

> "From the absoluteness of fundamental awareness
> Mind-as-such, a radiant light, (comes) the motility of original awareness;
> The pervasive stratum with the emotionally tainted ego-centred mind is spatiality,
> Motivation is motility, feeling temperature,
> Sensation cohesion, colour-form solidity.
> In this order we speak of product-process."[24]

Karma Phrin-las-pa uses the images of deep sleep, the restlessness of dream, and the event of waking up to illustrate the embodying process:[25]

> "In deep sleep all cognitive functions are gathered (suspended) in the pervasive stratum, and Mind-as-such, itself

a radiant light, is not moving. It is like a cloudless sky. Since the obscurations of the thought-constructions have not yet appeared, this mind radiant in itself is called 'motility of original awareness'. This does not mean that there is actual motility, but it is potentially there. It is like a great blankness. From this light there comes some darkness, that is to say, the light becomes slightly dim and, when sleep gets lighter, there is the stirring of the pervasive stratum with the emotionally tainted ego-centred mind, but as it is not recognized as what it is, it is spoken of as the motility of spatiality. From this dim light there comes diffusion, which means that darkness has become thicker and this means that from the pervasive stratum the ego-centred mind with its motivations rises. Since these motivations are stirring, as in a dream, there is the motility of motility. From the diffusion comes the settling (of final darkness). Motivation has become even more hardened. It is just like when we wake up, when feelings, sensations and perceptions corresponding to warmth, cohesion, and solidity, each exert their own motility. In brief, three kinds of motility in their order of dimming, diffusion, and darkness, derive each from the other or they manifest themselves as the five psychophysical constituents. This is meant by product-process."

In a similar vein Padma dKar-po describes embodiment as a loss of a peak or value experience. He quotes the *bDe-mchog rdo-rje mkha'-'gro*:

"The encompassed, the encompassing, a great openness,
Ever-present, irreducible,
Very open, plainly open.
This is without mind, there is no falling asleep
And no waking up.
There, there is no manifestation whatsoever."[26]

and then explains:

" 'The encompassed' is the concrete presence of the body, and 'the encompassing' is the radiant light. It is a 'great openness' as it is undivided like the flower and its fragrance.

It is 'ever-present' because it is like the sky everywhere. It is called the 'central pattern' because it serves as the bearer of its own presence in which the subject-object aberration of ordinary beings does not rise; it is called a non-conceptual motility because it is not diminished by something; it is a creative point because it is given as a spark of light. Since body, speech and mind cannot be split, it is 'irreducible'. As long as there is a moon, it will be reflected in the pool of the mind; thereby absolute non-existence is repudiated and since it does not appear as being (this or that) for ever, absolute existence is repudiated. It appears in dependent origination from its antecedent. Built up by various experientially initiated potentialities of experience since beginningless time, we may speak of it as 'mind', but as long as it is not free from the potentialities of actions and emotions it is a consciousness of all seeds, and therefore an 'appropriating consciousness'. The incessant splendour of what is called 'original awareness' is as the objective situation, the 'very open'; and as the owner of the objective situation 'the plainly open'. Since these three (aspects) are the reason for all that appears, the treatise says:

> From the brilliant light a great blankness,
> From this both enactment and appreciation come in a plurality (of life-forms).

Although in each individual there is this state of non-conceptuality (*rtog-med*) to be experienced, its non-recognition is like not recognizing the owner of a house when seeing him. The object, i.e., the owner of the house, and the subject, i.e., the beholder, are both not mistaken, and so the confusion of not recognizing the owner of the house is not tied to the object or subject. Therefore what exists does not appear to the beings and what does not exist appears. So Nāropa said:

> Ah, how wonderful, though non-existent (in themselves)
> The things of the three worlds appear.

Because there is appearance of what does not exist *per se* (the text declares):

I. A couple, Nāgārjunakoṇḍa (*Archaeological Survey of India*)

II. Two dancing couples, Nāgārjunakoṇḍa (*Archaeological*

Without mind, there is no falling asleep
And no waking up.

When confusion sets in, and this confusion is recognized for what it is, it submerges in the radiant light, like clouds in the sky dispersed by the wind. (Therefore)

There, there is no manifestation whatsoever."[27]

It is significant that this process of embodiment is said to be the quintessence of Saṃsāra. This shows that by embodiment not only my physical body is meant but my whole physical world as well. Saṃsāra is not something into which man has been 'thrown', an existentialist dictum that through Pascal's "Cast into the infinite immensity of spaces of which I am ignorant and which know me not, I am frightened" goes back to gnostic ideas; Saṃsāra is the continuously on-going act of embodiment, the existence or presence of my body being the primal condition for the existence and presence of the physico-cultural world. By means of its own organism, the mind experiences some particular milieu as structured in terms of its own particular intentions which are actualized by means of its bodily activities and always oriented towards the 'body' as the centre of this milieu. Since embodiment in the world is felt as a loss of Being, it can be retrieved, not by becoming absorbed in the source from which embodiment as a deficiency started but by rising above it; to use figurative language, by embodying Being. Embodied Being is termed *sku* (*kāya*), embodied loss of Being *lus* (*deha*). The English language has only one word for both terms: 'body'—a constant source of misunderstanding and misrepresentation of Tantric positive thought.

The Mind and the World of Appearance

In the same way as there is a difference between the body as lived by me, and the body imagined to be this or that kind of object for the various disciplines of science, there also is a difference in awareness between that for which we use the word 'mind' and that which often has been claimed to be a mysterious faculty in order to explain equally mysterious 'meanings' that were believed to be eternal essences or forms capable of being grasped by the 'mind'. But what is termed 'mind' in Tantrism is the recognition of an immanent power informing the wholeness of the universe and present everywhere together with it. It is not like the mentalistic postulate of a mind from which our world of appearance can be deduced. Emphasis is laid on experience which may come in many ways. Hence there are many terms, each of them indicative of the specific and subtle nuances which the experience may exhibit. We can understand some of these terms from a comparison of two broadly different types of perception. We can perceive anything and any person alternately in two different ways, sometimes as if he or it were the whole of all that is, but more often we perceive him or it as a part of the universe and related to the rest of it in complex ways, that is, we compare, contrast, approve, disapprove, categorize, classify. But we all resent being treated in this way, which we feel as a detraction from our being, and, precisely because we are in *need* of being recognized for what we really are, we try to command and extort this recognition which, of course, eludes us and merely reinforces the ego-centredness of ordinary perception; in the end it leads us farther and farther away from insightful perception and understanding and appreciation of what there is. sGam-po-pa indicates this by stating that

> "mind (*sems*) is ego-centred perception; a sentient being (*sems-can*) (is a term for) all beings (because they engage in ego-centred perception); but Mind-as-such (*sems-nyid*) is unceasing value-being (*chos-sku*)."[28]

This distinction between 'mind' and 'Mind-as-such', which is 'in' the body though not a derivative of it, does not endow the phenomenal universe or, in the narrower sense, the body with a 'spiritual' quality, but merely indicates the fact that man demonstrates in his own nature the potentiality of actualizing his Being which is 'absolute' in the sense that it cannot be reduced to some other kind of being, but not in the sense that it is something 'behind' or 'above' man. This innate pressure towards fuller and fuller Being is termed *bodhicitta* which, as we have seen in a previous chapter, is the very subtle in and of the body; it is simultaneously that which man is and that which he yearns and strives to be. Again, sGam-po-pa says:

> "If in order to attain Buddhahood the *bodhicitta* must precede it as cause-factor, in which cause-factor does this *bodhicitta* rest? In order to actualize the latter in ourselves we have to develop compassion and kindness. When we have become accustomed to them, the *bodhicitta* cannot but grow in us."[29]

Although sGam-po-pa speaks of a 'cause-factor' he does not understand by it some outside force that implants in man the ability to grow and 'press forward' his Being. The 'cause-factor' is the immanent and sustaining force that permits and helps what exists as a potentiality, to become actual. To understand 'mind' is 'to be' in an absolute sense and such being is an absolute value (*chos-sku*). Since Buddhahood is the realization of value-being, technically termed Dharmakāya, and since Dharmakāya is the realization of Mind-as-such, Buddhahood is the understanding of Mind-as-such. The growth of this understanding and awareness sGam-po-pa illustrates by the following simile:

> "Although the first phase of the moon is the moon, it is not capable to illumine (fully); although a lion cub is a

> lion, it cannot yet overpower the other (animals); and although a child is a human person, he has not yet the fullness of stature and strength."[30]

When Mind-as-such as a self-validating awareness is present, it carries its own intrinsic value with it, and the person who has it has a greater sense of being 'all-of-a-piece', of really being. In this way not only are Mind-as-such or absolute Awareness (*sems-nyid*) and Being-as-such-as-value (*chos-sku*) indivisible, so that it is correct to say that at this moment man is not divided against himself, but the awareness is of a field within which the parts exist to be subsequently discriminated by name; however, their existence is a free-floating 'let-be'. In other words, there is Being-as-such (*chos-sku*) with Mind-as-such (*sems-nyid*) with (its) field of Appearance-as-such (*snang-ba*). It is this unity of Being-Awareness-Appearance that sGam-po-pa is concerned with. He begins with Awareness and Appearance, the two poles in experience, and then gives them their existential interpretation of Being.[31]

> "Mind-as-such and togetherness are the two (poles). (With) Mind-as-such together value-being (*chos-kyi-sku*); (With) Appearance together value-being's light (*chos-sku'i 'od*).[32] '(With) Mind-as-such together value-being' means that (what we are concerned with) is beyond verbalizations, without colour and form, in itself uncreated. It cannot be objectified; it is all-encompassing like the sky; it is without conceptual fictions, unchanging, and (even) devoid of the voidness of an essence. '(With) appearance together value-being's light' means that, (while absolute Being) is without causes and conditions and without the ripple of the self-rising conceptual fictions, this (being together with appearance) constitutes the multitude of positive, negative and neutral fictions, which come incidentally.
>
> "Are these two (poles) one or different? Although they seem to be different to those who do not understand, they are one for those who understand through the instruction of the teacher. It is with them as with sandal wood and sandal-scent, sun and sun beams, water and waves. Al-

though the scent of sandal wood spreads into all directions, it does not part from the sandal wood; although the rays of the sun travel into the ten directions, they do not part from the sun; the waves do not part from the water. Similarly appearance does not part from Mind-as-such, nor does the latter from the former.

"There are three explanatory instances. One has to know (1) that the plurality (of the phenomenal universe) has risen from a source that is nothing in itself; (2) that although there is the plurality (of the phenomenal universe), this is nothing in itself; and that (3) when one understands it one cannot speak even of non-duality.

"Here the source that is nothing in itself is Mind-as-such being together (with appearance). The presence of the plurality (of the phenomenal universe) is Appearance being together (with Mind-as-such). Although there is this plurality (of the phenomenal universe) which is nothing in itself, nevertheless there does exist a plurality of conceptual fictions which are not realities in themselves. Not to be able to speak of non-duality when one understands it, means that the understanding of appearance and of its understanding as not being two cannot be represented in words, like the dream of a mute or a small child.

"There are three aspects in experiencing this. First, to relax in body and mind by not making strenuous efforts, then to rest in a state of genuineness by not harbouring doubts, and lastly, to recognize all feeling-supported fictions as 'unborn'.[33] When one actually goes about (this realization), body and mind are relaxed due to the absence of strenuous efforts, and when one has become without the fiction extending over the three aspects of time due to the absence of doubt, one is settled in the genuine presence (of Reality), and in the subsequent awareness whatever fictions appear are known as a former acquaintance, which is to say, one knows them as 'unborn'.

"In view of the necessity of 'sealing' (one's view of life with this experience) there are three supporting instructions: Since what is (called) 'togetherness existing in the Being of all beings', exists in its own right (in ourselves), it need not be searched for elsewhere. Since value-being, i.e., great bliss, in which no frustration is found, is a self-validating awareness, it is nowhere else (but in its awareness). Since the phenomenal universe is one's own mind, one's mind need not be afraid of itself and so one can dismiss anxiety and timidity.

"Furthermore, that which exists in (and as) the Being of all beings applies to all six kinds of beings and since the awareness of togetherness is all-encompassing, it need not be searched for anywhere else. 'No frustration' means that the frustration (inherent in) Saṃsāra has dissolved in the realm of the absolutely real; since absolute Being, great bliss, is (our) self-validating awareness, there is nothing else but Mind-as-such. Since the phenomenal universe is our mind, one (can) know everything as mind, and this as a radiant light, and this as the absolutely real. When one stays in the sphere of mind (as) the absolutely real, even if all beings were to become *devaputramāras*,[34] they would not find a chance to harm us, because the harming *devaputramāra* is the absolutely real itself and the absolutely real cannot harm itself. Therefore look at anxiety and timidity as the absolutely real."

From a purely philosophical point of view sGam-po-pa's statement, that the phenomenal universe is mind, is hardly tenable and many objections have been raised against it. Certainly, an experience may be a mental event, but what I experience is not for this reason mental. However, the philosophical objection against sGam-po-pa's statement detracts from sGam-po-pa's intention. He points to the experience of Being, but does not reduce its vividness to categories of discursive treatment. The 'is' in his statement therefore is not the 'is' of identity. He refers to the 'intuitive' or aesthetic aspect of perceiving which is 'timeless' since only the discursive treatment of the parts in and of the vision is subject to time. There would be no world if it were not for this power of seeing things together, and 'together' means more than just the parts of some object, it also means to be brought face-to-face with the world: I am with my world.

Significantly sGam-po-pa points out that in this experience the individual is free of the past and of the future in the special sense of an 'all-now' and 'all-here' and that this experience is felt to be characteristically positive. The standard term for this positive feeling is 'great bliss' (*mahāsukha*) where 'great' means that nothing could be greater than this. So also the character of light indicates a glow from within, but 'within' is merely a manner of speech since here the distinction between'within' and 'without', 'behind', 'above' are metaphors, not metaphysical entities. Another aspect is the complete loss of anxiety and fear which implies that perception is more open and less distorted and that the feeling of frustration has gone into abeyance. Lastly, until the ordinary way of perceiving reasserts itself and we begin to see everything, ourselves included, embedded in relationship with everything else and judge everything in relation to our self-centredness, whatever we perceive is perceived in the same way as when we meet a friend. There is no hostility whatsoever involved.

It is a sign of deep insight that when the 'three manifestations'[35] begin to operate and to constitute our ego-centred psychic life, the first 'quality' is hostility (*zhe-sdang*), for hostility or, in a less pronounced way, resentment functions as a strengthening of the sense of I-ness and sets the subject *against* the object, destroying their togetherness. Hostility also is the compelling force of every kind of dominance psychology, to gain power over others. There is a good deal of ambiguity in such hostility, as it may masquerade as 'possessive love' (*'dod-chags*) which, of course, is not love at all because in its possessiveness it denies the very Being of the other. While hostility generates the urge to conquer the 'object', possessive love generates the dependence of the subject on the object which is chiefly something to be clung to. And in the end there is the actual human situation (*rang-bzhin*), where everything has become a problem and frustration prevails, so aptly termed Saṃsāra—'moving in circles'.

Another term used in this connection is *'khrul-pa* (*bhrānti*), often translated by 'error'. But unlike our 'error', the Indian-

Tibetan term does not imply any culpability; it refers to a movement away from the real, a going astray into the world of 'appearance'. It seems as if here again the same distinction is made as we do when we speak of 'appearance' and contrast it with 'reality'. But there is no such thing as 'appearance' and 'reality'. The world really *is* what experience shows it to be. When we say that something is 'apparent' we are contrasting it with what would be or is disclosed in other experiences. For instance, I know that what I perceive in aesthetic experience of a table is in some sense the same table about which I may reflect intellectually. It is this latter way of perceiving that is termed *'khrul-pa*, which means to contaminate my aesthesis with intellectual abstractions, and therefore is a confused way of perceiving. While most of what 'appears' is in ordinary perception entangled with 'error', it is nevertheless possible to make the following distinction: all 'error' entails appearance, but not all appearance is 'error', because there is aesthetic immediacy, pure and uncontaminated (*dag-snang*). In this immediacy, what I perceive, be it a thing or a person, I perceive as meaningful, embodying significations of a determinate kind: it is *in* the blush that I perceive shame, *in* the pallor fear, and *in* the smile cheerfulness. There is no inferring from something presented (colour-form) to something not presented (shame, fear, cheerfulness). But not only do I perceive others, aesthetically and intellectually, I also perceive myself as perceiving with and by means of my body which, as we have seen, is an orientational centre for the spatio-temporal world. It is not a mere pun when it is said that appearance has an apparitional character:

> "In seeing appearance as an apparition, there is an apparitional body; by knowing that an apparition is 'open' (nothing in itself), there is the radiant light. These two are not two different things but form a unity",[36]

says sGam-po-pa. Actually, the difference between 'appearance' and 'apparition' is that the former is more descriptive, while the latter indicates how we experience appearance.

Togetherness is the key to understanding the unitary character of whatever experience we have. At one and the same time we have three separate ideas:

(i) aesthetic experience is the ground, and the *terminus a quo*, for all experience;

(ii) aesthetic experience is the path which distinguishes within itself the aesthetically convincing from the aesthetically unconvincing;

(iii) aesthetic experience is the goal. Unlike (i) which may exist only at the first instant in consciousness, easily lost in a 'downward pull' this (iii) is a definite attitude towards life.

Emphasis on aesthetic experience must not mislead us into the assumption that Tantrism is a kind of aestheticism by which a person or the world is placed on a mysterious pinnacle that does not exist. Aesthetic perception does not reveal 'mysterious' entities, but individual realities. These are termed *chos-nyid* or 'the absolutely real'. It is, so to speak, the whole of Being, and it is seen as if it were all there is in the universe, and it is fully attended to in its intrinsic uniqueness. This ground from which we can develop not only a greater aesthetic perception but also a kind of rubricizing-categorical perception, is termed Mahāmudrā,[37] and sGam-po-pa discusses the three aspects of aesthetic experience as follows:[38]

"There are here three phases: the ground in its uncontaminated (state), the path in its uncontaminated (operation), and the goal in its uncontaminated (attainment). The first is the 'absolutely real' (*chos-nyid*), uniquely pure. The second is to make togetherness-awareness the path, and the third is the indivisibility of the (aesthetic) field and its awareness.

"In order to make this uncontaminated and far-reaching state our way (of spiritual development) the 'Lotus' instruction is offered. The reference to the 'uncontaminated' is the mind in its state of being uncontaminated by (the postulate of) a subject and an object. The instruction in making the 'far-reaching' our way is to make the path proceed from the starting-point (ground) which is the attainment of uncontaminatedness. This is like a lotus-flower. Although it grows in the mud, its stem, leaves and flowers are not affected by the mud. Similarly, having the ground, uncontaminated and being a togetherness, brought into perspective (*lta-ba*) by attending to it and making an experience of it, the path, uncontaminated and being the radiant light, is travelled, and the goal, uncontaminated and being value-being (*chos-sku*), is attained. The 'Lotus' instruction which is the means has four topics:

"(i) The adoption of the Mahāmudrā as a perspective through which the Mahāmudrā is seen as uncontaminated and far-reaching. That is to say: the whole universe has risen as appearance through 'togetherness-awareness'. This (togetherness) is of three kinds: (*a*) 'outward togetherness', (*b*) inward togetherness, and (*c*) mystical togetherness.

"(*a*) All that appears as the objects for the six perceptual processes (sensory and intellectual) of an externalized world is together with the 'absolutely real', and the 'absolutely real', which is nothing-as-such, is together with appearance. These two are together in the sense that neither is earlier or later and that neither is concretely good or evil. Thus Saraha said:

> Understand appearance to be the teacher;
> Understand the plurality (of the phenomenal world) as
> having one flavour;
> Let things be together.

As long as we do not understand this togetherness we harbour ideas (fiction) that external objects are there to be grasped (by a mind), but when we understand it we speak of this (awareness) as togetherness-awareness in its intrinsic nature, that is an aesthetically perceptive awareness of a plurality in terms of objective situation and owner of the objective situation.

"(*b*) The internal cognitive process exists together with the radiant light, which is nothing-as-such, and this Mind-as-such, the radiant light, nothing-as-such, exists together with the internal cognitive process. These, (too), are together in the sense that neither is earlier nor later and that neither is concretely good or evil. As long as this togetherness is not understood there is the idea (fiction) of an internal cognitive process but, when it is understood, we speak of togetherness-awareness in its intrinsic nature, that is an aesthetically perceptive awareness of a plurality in terms of objective situation and owner of the objective situation. Similarly Saraha said:

The fictions are absolute awareness;
The five poisons[39] are medicine;
The concept of an object and the concept of a subject
are both Vajradhara.

"(*c*) The cognitive act that does away with overevaluation and underestimation exists together with the absolutely real aesthetic field. As long as it is not understood, we have (still the idea of a) togetherness-awareness but, when it is understood, the last trace of any conceptual fiction in intrinsic awareness is removed by the onset of this field-awareness. This indivisibility of aesthetic field and awareness is variously termed 'pure awareness' or 'conceptless awareness'. Actually there is nothing that might be termed 'awareness'. So also Saraha said:

'No path, no awareness'."

This last statement is meant to abolish any attempt to conceptualize Being-as-such which, as we have seen, is synonymous with absolute Awareness or Mind-as-such. The moment we attribute a certain predicate to Being or Awareness, we are conceptualizing it; we have a concept of something and we attribute to Being the characteristic of which we have the concept. Actually, therefore, we can say nothing at all about Being, and all that we say can only be a means to help us to find out Being, and this is to travel the path. It is equally clear that this aesthetic awareness is not determined by its content; as a matter of fact it does not matter what the content is. Similarly, sGam-po-pa's statement that this togetherness is neither good nor evil shows that the state of a moral agent's mind does not matter, but only what he does in a moral situation. There is of course a connection between what we may call aesthetic and moral awareness in Tantrism. The point is first to see the other in his or her Being, not through the distorting opinions that are the loss of Being-awareness, be this of oneself or of others. Thus again it is insight and knowledge that is of primary importance, and whether we like it or not because of vested interests, morality is still grounded in knowledge. I am morally responsible only for having done what I *know* I ought not to have done and for not having done what I *know* I ought to have done. Just as opinion is the travesty of knowledge, so morality based on opinion with its dogmatism is a travesty of morality. Man not only *is*, he also acts, and in order to act according to his Being he has to attend to it. Therefore sGam-po-pa continues:[40]

> "It is not enough to bring the things of this world into perspective as being together (with our awareness of them), we have to experience their (being) by fully attending to it. This is 'to know how to make the radiant light which is uncontaminated the way (of one's spiritual development)'. That is to say, the whole phenomenal universe has from its very beginning been the actuality of the radiant light, nothing-as-such, unborn, absolute value-being, free from the limitations of assertions about it. As has been said in a Śūtra,
>
> 'Profound, peaceful, wordless, radiant, uncreated.'
>
> When the universe is thus understood as unborn, one settles in the sphere where no subjectivism obtains, since one has freed oneself from the contaminations such as attention, non-attention, existence, non-existence, and so forth. The Great Brahmin (Saraha) declared:
>
> 'The absolutely and uniquely real is without words,
> Let (its) cognition be without conceptualizations.'
>
> And,
>
> 'Let the fresh cognition be (spontaneous) like a child.' "

While man demonstrates in his own nature a pressure towards realizing his Being, there is another force pulling at him, leading to stagnation, repression, fixation, and, above all, frustration. This opposing force is 'unknowing' (*avidyā*, *ma-rig-pa*) which, as sGam-po-pa informs us, is the obverse of the 'togetherness-awareness'.[41] This means that 'mind' is a potentiality that may move either way. Graphically this would be:

Being ←——→ Knowledge ←——→ Buddha

↑

(body—) MIND (—body)

↓

ordinary person ←→ opinion ←→ postulated (fictional) being

This unknowing is itself the outcome of inveterate tendencies which find their expression in concepts (*rnam-rtog*)[42] which are due to our actions and our emotional responses, leaving traces that themselves are potentialities of similar experiences. This is characteristic of the ordinary person who is 'tossed about' by the storm of his emotions. Specifically, concepts curtail the possibility of fully cognizing by abstracting from the immediate experience, by selecting some attributes, rejecting others, and distorting still others. They also tend to relate the aspects of the object to our linguistic system which is, of course, unable to deal with the ineffable. This, if it is forced into words, is at once changed and made into something other than it is. However, when an ordinary person looks at a tree, he engages in both aesthetic and conceptual activity, but he does not keep these two activities pure, and since his life is largely superficial and little more than what he can talk about, the conceptual framework is all he cares about. *But* the concepts are not something over and above 'appearance'. Thus sGam-po-pa correctly observes:[43]

> "All that appears and can be talked about is (dealt with by) concepts. Without concepts there cannot be any 'appearance'; concepts are the mind. The mind is unborn, and the unborn is openness (nothing-as-such).[44] Openness is the absolutely and uniquely real. The absolutely and uniquely real that is not something or other is the presence of the plurality (of the phenomenal world). When this plurality is present, it has not parted from what is nothing-as-such. When you understand how the two truths (absolute and relative) are indivisible, you have brought the things of this world into perspective. When you maintain this perspective, you are fully attentive. The result is the abolishment of hope and fear."

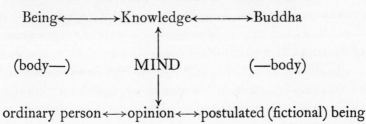

Any presentation, whether philosophic, scientific, or instructional, is a body of propositions, and a body of propositions is a set of concepts. If it were not for concepts we would be unable to communicate and even to know.[45] Moreover, there are different kinds of concepts and each, in a certain sense, is an 'abstraction' because the immediately apprehendable lends itself to 'abstractions', that is, constructs of the mind.[46] Usually we tend to restrict concepts to the differentiations in and abstractions from the totality of the aesthetic presence, and therefore we have failed to recognize that from which the abstractions have been made. When the idea of pure perception is said to be 'without concepts' (*mi-rtog-pa*), this does not imply an utter blankness or the proverbial emptiness of the mind, rather the full appreciation of the totality from which subsequently abstractions can be made as if they were the only reality, enmeshing us in a self-proliferating and self-frustrating game of hide-and-seek; but the same concepts may also be helpful and pointers to what is ever-present, the self-creativity of the mind which I experience as embodying itself in my body or in the concepts or constructs of the mind. The full appreciation and awareness of Being is not reducible to and caught in the abstractions, and it is this irreducibility that is indicated by 'concept-less awareness' (*mi-rtog-pa'i ye-shes*). sGam-po-pa has this to say about the concept as the mind's manifestation in the same way that the mind is a manifestation of Being:[47]

> "Concepts are to be seen as a benefactor, not as dispensable. They are to be seen as a necessity, as a beloved. Concepts are just concepts. They are friends; they are the way; they are fuel to appreciative discrimination. (*a*) They are not discovered by looking for them (in some hidden place) and by ferreting them out; (*b*) they do not take up residence somewhere; and (*c*) they are not (subjective) interpretations.
>
> "(*a*) This means that whatever rises in reason (*blo*) is to be considered as concept; concepts are to be considered as the working of the mind (*sems*); and this working which is unborn is to be considered as absolute Being (*chos-sku*).
>
> "Beginners should use positive concepts to banish negative ones, but (the following should be borne in

mind): If the sun is covered by clouds, these may be white or black. Similarly, if a person is fettered, he may be fettered by an iron chain or a gold chain. By way of analogy, one may be fettered by positive concepts and by negative ones. Both kinds are to be considered as the working of the mind, and this working, unborn, is to be considered as absolute Being. This is openness in action.

"(*b*) When by examining all concepts the noetic capacity has exhausted itself, concepts do not take up their stay in death, or in man, or in openness. All these conditions are to be considered as concepts, and these are to be considered as the working of the mind, and this working, unborn, is absolute Being.

"(*c*) This means the (concepts) must not be interpreted as suchness, as the way, or as the goal: not even as perspective, attention, or enactment. Reason (*blo*) falling in with (concepts) is (in itself) an utter openness. This means that (*a*) concepts can be overcome the moment they arise, (*b*) they can be overcome later; and (*c*) they can be like a spreading fire.

"(*a*) This is like meeting a former acquaintance—the moment a concept rises it is recognized as absolute Being.

"(*b*) This is like meeting an unknown person, or like snow falling on a lake. The moment the snow falls on a lake it does not melt, only afterwards. Not knowing the concept one may first seek it out and later one will know it.

"(*c*) This is like a forest fire. As long as it is small, the wind and so on will kill it, but the bigger it grows, the wind, however powerful, will aid it. Similarly one should attend to concepts as if one had been grossly insulted, as if one had been infected by leprosy, or as if one has met a great misfortune. (In so doing) one should consider them as concepts; the concepts as the working of the mind, and this working, unborn, as absolute Being. Attention to them in this way, is devotion (to turn the negative into the positive), no-erring, and an opening of the door to reality by appreciative discrimination.

" 'Devotion' means: When one knows one concept to be absolute Being, one knows all concepts to be so. Just as when one has drunk the water of one lake, one knows the water of all lakes; or when one knows one cane to be hollow, one knows all canes to be hollow; or when one knows one germ to attack the marrow, one knows all germs to do so. 'To turn the negative into the positive' means: when one has purified one's mind as if by a raging fire, all unfavourable conditions become one's friend.

" 'No-erring' means that as long as one has not recognized the concepts for what they are, there is erring. When one has gone to the root of the concepts, and recognized them as absolute Being, there is no reason for going astray anymore.

" 'Opening the door' means: like brandishing a lance in the open air, everything is understood as being identical with itself."

III. A couple, Nāgārjunakoṇḍa (*Archaeological Survey of India*)

IV. A couple, Nāgārjunakoṇḍa (*Archaeological Survey of India*)

Ecstatic Bliss and Emotional Entanglement

We have seen that Tantrism distinguishes between the body as lived by me and constituting a value, and the body as conceived as an object of speculation; between mind as a potentiality and potency, and mind as a comprehensive term for ego-centred tendencies; between absolute cognitiveness and the world of concepts. This same division applies to the realm of feeling and emotions and is also borne out by experience. A person in a peak-experience of, say, pure aesthetic perception and enjoyment feels himself at his best and fullest. He feels more perceptive and contented than at other times, but the feeling he experiences defies categorization. Not only is this ecstatic bliss felt subjectively but it can be seen by others who may, however, fail to understand what is going on in the person who has this experience. We have only to remind ourselves of the Buddha's meeting with the Ājīvika Upaka who remarks of the Buddha that he looks so happy and so radiant, and who cannot understand what the Buddha says about his experience.[48]

The feeling-tone of this experience is termed *mahāsukha*, which literally translated means 'great pleasure', and 'great' again is used to indicate its absolute character, while 'pleasure' is no ordinary pleasure; but since pleasure has a positive connotation because it is a life-enhancing state, this term is used for indicating the absolutely positive character of the experience, cognitively unlimited and emotionally satisfying. We may use such phrases as 'ecstatic bliss' or 'great bliss', or 'absolute bliss' to refer to the sense of freedom from the impoverishment brought about by ego-centredness.

In the same way that emphasis is laid on Being-as-value (*sku*) and cognitive potentiality (*ye-shes*) rather than on one's physical and imaginary being (*lus*) and one's conceptualization about Being (*rnam-rtog*), 'ecstatic bliss' figures prominently in Tantric thought. Its association with the awareness of Being shows that Tantrism is not hedonism which is a veiled form of libertinism and its contempt for the world.

Indrabhūti declares:[49]

"The All-Buddha-Awareness which is experienced within ourselves
Is called Great Bliss because it is the most excellent pleasure of all pleasures."

Advayavajra states:[50]

"Without bliss there is no enlightenment, for enlightenment is bliss itself."

Anangavajra says:[51]

"It is thought of as sublime Great Bliss, because it is by nature infinite pleasure;
It is most sublime, all-good, conducive to and of the same nature as enlightenment."

Here 'conducive', which as a technical term implies connaturality, can only mean that in this state ever new riches are discovered.

Kāṇha says:[52]

"The whole world, together with its deeds, words, and thoughts, vanishes into this air.
This vanishing is Great Bliss, the same as Nirvāṇa."

Here, too, the equation of bliss and Nirvāṇa indicates the positive character of the experience. Historically, it is a restatement of the Buddha's words that Nirvāṇa is bliss because it is not a judgment (conceptualization) of feeling having a pleasurable tone.

Saraha declares:[53]

"Just as in deep darkness the moon-stone spreads its light,
So this supreme Great Bliss in a moment dissipates all misery."

Again we see here the intimate connection between bliss as the highest form of pleasurable excitement and the radiance of an alive person. The imagery of the moon-stone spreading its light effortlessly aptly illustrates the fact that while we 'struggle' to get away from the painfulness of a disturbing situation, we just 'flow out' to pleasure.

gNyis-med Avadhūtipa explains Saraha's verse as follows:[54]

> "The veil of emotionality and conceptualization is like livid darkness. It is dispelled by the teaching of the true Guru[55] who is like the moon-stone found in the world of the Nagas, and who makes understood what has not been understood. Hence (Saraha says): 'Just as in deep darkness the moon-stone. . . .' Just as the moon-stone need not take the darkness away to some other place, so also it is not necessary to reject emotionality and conceptualizations (they just disappear). Hence (Saraha continues): 'Spreads its light.'
>
> "Since in a single moment, immediately after this sublime and uncommon Great Bliss, not sullied by the mire of Saṃsāra and Nirvāṇa, has been pointed out, the meaning of Buddhahood is seen, (Saraha declares): 'So this supreme Great Bliss in a moment. . . .'
>
> "Subjectivism is the evil of thinking; non-subjectivism is the happiness of concentration. The concepts deriving from 'memory'[56] weary mind out, but by experiencing 'non-memory', subjectivism is conquered. (Hence Saraha concludes): 'Conquers all the evil of thinking.' "

Karma Phrin-las-pa[57] interprets this verse as referring to the existential value of being (*sku*) which is felt as, and hence termed, 'bliss'. He says:

> " 'Deep darkness' is a darkness in which there is no light. It has been accumulated through aeons. When then the moon, or the jewel of the sky, the sun, spread their light, simultaneously with the birth of light the darkness is annihilated. When the understanding of this supreme Great Bliss, Mahāsukha, dawns, simultaneously and instantaneously 'all the evil of thinking' that has been accumulated since beginningless Saṃsāra 'is conquered'. Therefore the whole of karmic activity and of emotionality

has been eradicated. 'The evil of thinking' means that (categorical) thinking is evil and evil is (categorical) thinking; it creates a veil. 'All' means the seeds and tendencies of this veiling power. In the same way as pleasure is contrasted with pain, the original awareness from which all veiling power, together with its latent potentialities has disappeared, is called in the Vajrayāna 'the existential value of bliss'. And this is meant here."

Here Being and Awareness are used synonymously. Being is a value of highest significance; it also is an Awareness, not an absorption in something other than itself. However, the ambivalence which we have seen to pervade the whole of Tantric thought, is also evident in the contrast between 'bliss' and 'emotionality', the latter being a loss or distortion of the former rather than an independent opposing force. This is, according to the commentators, the intention of Saraha's words:

"O son, listen! By the various (concepts)
This flavour cannot be explained,
'Tis rather the rejection of the understanding of the stable bliss
(Which) is like the re-emergence of the fickle (mind)."[58]

To speak of Being and Awareness as Bliss affirms the existence of the highest value within man himself, to be discovered there and aiding the discovery. In other words, it is creative in a very special sense, that is, to see the world with a fresh vision and to approach life with open-eyed wonder, not with inhibitory and rigidly set presuppositions as is done by the person who gets caught in his own fictions. At the moment of bliss the person is more himself and more perceptive, he can appreciate and accept reality, and he will not try to make it conform to his illusions.

For most people the experience of bliss is a rare event and most of the time their life is felt to be frustrating. The Buddhist contention that 'everything is frustrating' (*sarvaṃ duḥkhaṃ*) is to be understood from this experience of bliss which coincided with the Buddha's enlightenment. It was only after this event that he formulated the 'Four Noble Truths' which, therefore, are not so much premises from which deductions may be made, but rather conclusions and descriptions of factual situations. From the fact that bliss and Nirvāṇa and enlightenment are synonymous, it is obvious that bliss is not merely the absence of pain and frustration. It is true, relief from pain and the solution of a problem often produces a feeling of pleasure, but this is a phenomenon on the rebound. The pain or the problem has made us conscious of a particular situation, and we are also conscious of the pleasure for a short time after its release or solution. As soon as the pain or problem is forgotten, the pleasure of release is also gone. It seems to be more correct to state that Bliss is the basic state of an integrated and healthy person, while fluctuating feelings of pleasure and pain denote some disturbance of this basic state and represent a loss of bliss and intrinsic awareness.

Basic to the frustration we encounter is the loss and lack of intrinsic awareness (*avidyā*, *ma-rig-pa*) which, as a distortion of original awareness and its blissful character, acts as a powerful emotion which sustains an equally distorted and strained activity which is consciously felt as frustrating. These three aspects of emotionality, strained activity, and the sense of frustration, are the first three members in the chain of dependent origination (*pratītyasamutpāda*) which in the history of Buddhist thought has found a variety of interpretations. According to the Tantric interpretation the lack of intrinsic awareness (*avidyā*) is basic to both the more positive emotions of attraction, attachment, love, and the more negative ones of aversion, hostility, hatred. It is unfortunate that every term can be used ambiguously and very often is used deceptively. Take for instance the word 'love'. It may refer to an experience of infinite richness in which the subject admires, adores and enjoys the other person or object as something intrinsically precious and worthy in its own right and for its own sake, but also to the tormenting irrationality of possessiveness, acquisitiveness and selfishness culminating in the perverse notion of 'sacrificial love', the love a killer feels for his victim.[59] Is there anything more terrifying than to picture oneself as the victim of some ritual murder; and is there anything more detestable than to inflict death on a living being for the mere satiation of the lust for blood or to destroy another person's happiness for the sake of self-aggrandizement? The love that admires and enjoys belongs to 'enlightenment', which is intrinsic awareness and bliss in one; the so-called love that disregards life and counts nothing as valuable reflects the distorted view we take of the world whose richness and beauty therefore elude us continuously. In the moment of 'enlightenment' we can be 'all-loving' and 'all-perceptive', and we are not swayed by conflicting emotions that lead to countless evils. Padma dkar-po says:[60]

> "The loss of intrinsic awareness (*ma-rig-pa*, *avidyā*) presents itself as unconducive to, and in contrast with, intrinsic awareness with its unchanging and absolute (feeling of) love. This loss is the moment that becomes the cause of birth and death for sentient beings. It associates with possessiveness due to the experientially initiated potentiality of possessiveness, present since beginningless time, and thus becomes attachment (*'dod-chags*, *rāga*). By changing, it loses its character of attachment and becomes aversion (*zhe-sdang*, *dveṣa*). The nature of aversion is blindness (lit. swoon), and this is (mental) darkness. Attachment, aversion, and mental darkness constitute the loss of intrinsic awareness, which then is an emotional force."

It is significant that aversion, not love, is explained as mental darkness. Although attachment may lead to dependence upon the other it still enables me to see more and even to know more of the other. Usually we say 'love is blind', precisely because by tradition we have associated everything positive with the Devil; but Buddhism, not suffering from a power-inflated straitjacket of dehumanizing dogmaticism, recognizes the observable fact that love can be more perceptive than non-love. On the other hand, aversion, hatred, malice, fury make us quite literally blind. We say 'blind with rage' and this negativity, in line with our nihilistic transcendentalism, we associate with God—the 'wrath of God' is a favourite topic of preachers who switch to the 'love of God' when it becomes a matter of concealing unpleasant facts and of perpetuating society's wrongs.

Emotionality, ambivalent in itself, sustains equally ambivalent actions which are judged as good or evil, and which, in turn, are motivating forces. Thus Padma dkar-po continues:[61]

> "Good and evil aroused by (emotionality) is motivation or karmic activity (*karma*)."

Such actions involve us in situations, and to become involved is like being conceived in a womb; we are caught in a situation and we perceive by way of classifying, conceptualizing, and, above all, comparing. All this is frustrating, because we perceive only part of what there is. Padma dkar-po continues:[62]

> "(Through karmic activity) to become 'en-wombed', is abstractive categorizing perception (*vijñāna*), which is frustration."

Emotionality (*kleśa*), karmic activity (*karma*) and the sense of frustration (*duḥkha*) underlie our embodied existence which is described by the remaining nine members of the chain of dependent origination, and which make it clear that we move from one situation to another, each situation, so to speak, being a new existence of ours. Among the remaining nine members three are always more intimately related to each other. Thus there is 'name and form' (*nāma-rūpa*) which refers to the sum total of the five psychophysical constituents with their 'six interactional fields' (*āyatana*) and the 'rapport' (*sparśa*) that exists between the perceiving act and the perceived content. Similarly, 'feeling' (*vedanā*), to estimate the pleasurable or painful relationship of some aspect of reality to oneself, 'craving' (*tṛṣṇā*), to have more of pleasant feeling and to get rid of unpleasant feelings, and 'appropriation' (*upādāna*), to have everything for oneself, are close together. Lastly, 'becoming' (*bhava*), to move into one of the possible life-forms, 'birth' (*jāti*), to be fully in a new situation, and 'old age and death' (*jarāmaraṇa*), belong together. The twelve members of this chain of dependent origination, divided into four groups of three, represent the distorted aspect of Being in the form of an individual and the way he goes about life. The individual is a triad in the sense that he exists by way of body (*lus*), speech (*ngag*) and subjective mind (*yid*).[63] Hence, emotionality, karmic activity, and the sense of frustration mark the individual's dynamic existence in various degrees of intensity. The following diagram will show the existential implication:

unknowing (*avidyā*) motivation (*saṃskārāḥ*) perception (*vijñāna*)	*jñānavajra* (cognitive being)
name and form (*nāma-rūpa*) fields of interaction (*ṣaḍāyatana*) rapport (*sparśa*)	*kāyavajra* (embodied being)
feeling (*vedanā*) craving (*tṛṣṇā*) appropriation (*upādāna*)	*vāgvajra* (communicative being)
becoming (*bhava*) birth (*jāti*) old age and death (*jarāmaraṇa*)	*cittavajra* (responsive being)

The first set of three is the presupposition of the individual's embodiment in Saṃsāra and is termed *ye-shes rdo-rje* (*jñānavajra*), 'the indestructibility (*rdo-rje*, *vajra*) of original awareness (*ye-shes*, *jñāna*); the second set is the actual embodiment and termed *sku rdo-rje*, (*kāyavajra*), 'the indestructibility of Being'. It is through man's embodied Being that he also communicates with the world, and so the third set is termed *gsung rdo-rje* (*vāgvajra*), 'the indestructibility of communication'. The last set is termed *thugs rdo-rje* (*cittavajra*), 'the indestructibility of responsiveness'. Not only is man in the world and not only does he communicate with it, he also responds to life and its challenges. This he can do either by remaining true to his Being or by being oblivious to it and becoming involved in the fictions of his own making in the wake of his loss of intrinsic awareness of Being. At first glance the correspondence between the four sets of three of the chain of dependent origination and the four 'indestructibilities' may seem to be artificial. However, the sense of frustration which inheres in all actions that derive from an imperfect view of reality, indicate that there can be insight, original awareness (*ye-shes*). Similarly the psychophysical constituents are abstractions from man's existence and point to his real Being (*sku*), and it is through our moods and judgments of feeling that we communicate (*gsung*) with other persons and the world around us. Although communication is mostly related to words, more important is the timbre of the voice which clearly reflects my mood, and my mood may colour the whole situation. Lastly, in becoming I respond to the possibilities that the situation offers. The response is to what becomes my life-world and again I respond to it totally. Thus potentiality leads to actuality which in the last analysis points to and remains a potentiality, which at the same time is the capacity to affirm the values by which we live. Such values are existential; they are not the products of intellectual rationalizations through which they may be dimly seen and which may spur us on to find the values that are our very Being. According to this view good and evil take on a new meaning. They are not entities defined once and for all to choose between, but approximations to and alienations from the ultimate value that is Being and Awareness in one. This is the interpretation which Mi-pham gives of a sentient being (*sems-can*), that is, a person who has (*-can*) a mind (*sems*) and has intentions in the light of his limited perspective, in contrast with 'original awareness' (*ye-shes*) which is Buddhahood. This explanation is so much more revealing as it also clarifies the technical terms Dharmakāya and Rūpakāya whose exact meanings have baffled students of Buddhism. Dharmakāya is a term for Being-as-such, experienced as an absolute value; Rūpakāya is its representation in a perceptible way, that is, through being a Nirmāṇakāya man represents the ultimate value of Being, and through simultaneously being a Sambhogakāya he is empathetically one with the ultimate value of Being. Mi-pham says:[64]

> " 'Sentient being' (*sems-can*) is merely the self-manifesting deviation from the sphere of the radiant light. In this deviate manifestation improvement by good (deeds) and deterioration by evil (deeds) work infallibly. On the basis of this (division) there are merits and demerits. By abandoning evil and strengthening good we have the so-called 'accumulation of merits'. Through them we temporarily realize the happiness and prosperity of a god, a human being, or a Bodhisattva, and ultimately the Rūpakāya.[65]
>
> " 'Original awareness' is a term applied to non-deviation by having understood the absolutely real quite concretely.

> By this awareness the two veils (of emotionality and conceptuality) are torn and the goal, Dharmakāya, is realized. This is so stated in the *hetuyāna*.[66] In the *mantrayāna*[67] one understands that when the initial radiant light has been made one's foundation, the deviate manifestation dissolves by itself and there is no place for improvement by good and deterioration by evil."

According to this passage to be a sentient being is a 'deviation' (*'khrul-pa*, *bhrānti*). The original term has often been falsely translated as 'error'. More appropriate would have been 'alienation' which is an ancient psychiatric term meaning loss of personal identity or the feeling of personal identity. Since 'personal identity' may be too subjectively toned, the meaning of alienation can be restated as an on-going loss of and deviation from one's Being. Devoid of all spontaneity and all joy in living, the person is a stranger to himself and all his activity seems to him to belong not to himself but to an alien and dark power that holds sway over him and at whose bidding he goes about his work. Yet this estrangement from himself is very much resented by him. He recognizes it as unnatural and wants to emancipate himself from it, to regain himself. The alienated man is controlled by his emotions (*kleśa*), the compulsive activity (*karma*) initiated by them, and the accompanying sense of frustration (*duḥkha*) because whatever he does falls short of what he expects to be the outcome. Already in the earliest Buddhist writings, the Pāli Canon, we find accurate descriptions of the alienated person contrasted with the peak-experience of emancipation:[68]

> "The cycle of existence is of unknown origin. No beginning is known for the beings who run and move (from one existence to another), hindered (to recognize their true Being) by their lack of intrinsic awareness and fettered by the craving (for continued existence). For this reason, frustration has been experienced for a long time; pain and decay have been experienced and the cremation ground has been filled."

Here two factors have been mentioned together; lack of intrinsic awareness and craving. The latter term can also be rendered by 'drive' as a convenient term to describe a certain early temporal phase in adjustive activity going on between a state of disequilibrium and one of balance, which may be termed an end or a goal. The attainment of the goal by the reduction of tension or the satisfaction of the craving generally leads to a state of equilibrium, which is accompanied by a sense of pleasure and relaxation. But as long as the craving remains unsatisfied, and unfulfilled, a residuum of unpleasant feeling, however small it may be, remains and a new cycle of activity will ensue, and its first stage is a need, a longing, a want or a drive resulting from the disequilibrium. The association of 'craving' with 'lack of intrinsic awareness' emphasizes the inability to adjust oneself to the demands of life and denotes the state of imbalance and ambiguousness together with the ensuing drive, in the proper sense of the word, as well as the initial seeking of the stimulus or the situation which will satisfy this need. The attempt to avoid the tension which is felt as negative, and to secure the reduction of tension anticipated as positive, fails as long as man is dominated by opinions which are the quintessence of the lack of intrinsic awareness and have an overpowering emotional character. People have been known to have been tortured and killed for not sharing in the opinion someone has voiced (religious persecution and political assassination are still with us and often go together).

The overpowering force of the drive is well expressed in the following words:[69]

> "I shall describe craving to you, the ensnarer, a stream, diffused and tenacious, whereby the world is assailed and overwhelmed, entangled like a ball of string, and covered with blight; it becomes a jungle of Muñja (Saccharum munja Roxb.) and Pabbaja (Bleusine indica) grass and does not pass beyond lowly forms of life, sorrowful existence, ruin, and the cycle of rebirths."

And the moving on from one situation to another is stated as follows:[70]

> "Accompanied by craving, man goes a long way,
> He does not pass beyond Saṃsāra, existence here, existence there."

By way of contrast, the peak-experience (*agga*) is characterized by the disappearance of this driving force:[71]

> "Whatever there may be of concrete or abstract (things) it is the dispassionateness towards them that is called the peak-experience. It is a disintoxication, a fading of craving, break-up of the foundation, the destruction of the cycle of rebirth, the waning of craving, dispassionateness, delight in a peak-experience."

Dispassionateness (*virāga*) is not a loss of feeling, rather it is a heightened perceptivity in love and compassion (*mahārāga*); gone is the ego-centred feeling of possessiveness with its anxieties, fears, and inhibitions.

Because of the importance of the role of drives in the ordinary life of a person, Buddhism has dwelt upon this problem at length. As we know, in some drive-to-goal relationships there is essentially an effort to secure more and more of the satisfying stimulus or situation until release of the disturbing tensions or of the state of disequilibrium is attained. Thus, for instance, an organism, though incited by disturbing tensions and drives, by the process of reflex circular action continues to absorb more and more of the satisfying stimulus, as in eating and drinking. Also the whole range of love reactions takes on this character, from the tactile stimulation of the erogenous areas of the body to the other items in the love life of the adults. In the same way, training in social contacts leads to a continued desire for companionship and for the other things of which we are accustomed to say 'the more we get the more we want'. This continuation shows that there is still some unpleasant feeling-emotional tone. The effort was to avoid the more negative situation and to secure the less negative situation. These drives, which continue even after the consummatory response, are called attractional, and this sort of repetition falls under the head of perseverance. In the Buddhist text the two terms 'craving for continued existence' (*bhavataṇhā*) and 'craving for pleasure' (including sex, *kāmataṇhā*) are used for our concepts of attraction and perseverance. Buddhaghosa speaks of these two concepts in the following way:[72]

> " 'The craving for the objects' (*rūpataṇhā*) is called 'craving

> for pleasure' (*kāmataṇhā*), when an object comes into the range of visual consciousness and when this craving continues to absorb the object because of its pleasurable stimulus (i.e., attraction). But when this craving is continued with the idea of permanence, (that is, when the subject desires that) the object should be lasting and eternal, then it is called 'craving for continued existence' (*bhavataṇhā*) (i.e., perseverance), for a desire accompanied by the idea of permanence is called 'craving for continued existence'."

However, even then most attractive stimuli lose their appeal with persistent presentation and absorption. One tires in time of love making. Repeated contact with people leads to a state of discomfort and one wants to be alone for a time. In other words, the satiation of an attractional drive often leads to a shift from attraction to avoidance. There is a distinct limit to perseverance. Avoidance has been termed 'craving for discontinuance' (*vibhavataṇhā*).

Buddhaghosa says:[73]

> "When (this craving) is accompanied by the idea of annihilation, (that is when the subject desires that) the object should break up and perish, then it is called 'craving for discontinued existence' (*vibhavataṇhā*); for the desire accompanied by the idea of annihilation is called 'craving for discontinued existence'."

In the same way as an attractional drive may become an avoidant drive, so also the more avoidant drives may change their meaning for the individual. Society, culture, ideas, and learning constantly interfere with and qualify the drives and cycles of activity. Therefore it is not at all an easy thing to define a drive in terms of attraction or avoidance. A further complication is that in course of time the individual learns to thrust some of his anticipatory activities into the future as the basis of a line of action. These are referred to as ideals, but when we talk of them, we are but stating in another way the principle of an internal, goal-directed drive. These ideals, moreover, serve to set off many cycles of long-term activity which may be finally ended when many years have elapsed. But it should never be forgotten that the deeply perseverative character of many of our drives, whether we think of them in connection with long-term cycles of activity or of the many subsidiary cycles, may rather obviously prevent an efficient adaptation, not only to a particular situation but also to the final goal, whatever this may be. The inertia of our habitual pattern is all too evident, and it is always up to the individual to overcome this inertia in some way or other. We establish habits in order to escape the time- and effort-consuming procedure of applying our mental gifts to new tasks. The function of habits in our lives is primarily to do away with the faint vestige of spiritual growth. How strong the inclination to stagnate is in man, becomes most evident when we analyze beliefs. The core of every belief is prejudice. Swayed by emotions we make an unjustified generalization. Habits which prevent us from applying new knowledge impair our spiritual growth considerably. We tend to become static and to deal with states of Being, and by introducing a (conceptual) split in Being we try to play the one against the other: either this or that, or nothing. But negativism in any form is not a solution. Candrakīrti clearly says that the either-or ends in failure:[74]

> "Those who try to solve the problems of life either by continuation (*bhava*) or by discontinuation (*vibhava*) have no true knowledge. Both extremes have to be given up; the attractional drive (*bhava tṛṣṇā*) as well as the avoidant drive (*vibhava tṛṣṇā*)."

The distinction between an ordinary person and a Buddha, as indicated by the descriptive terms *sems-can* 'having a mind', and *mkhyen-pa* 'being aware in an original way', and the philosophical terms *sems* 'mind' and *sems-nyid* 'Mind-as such', points to an important observation. The term *sems*, which is usually rendered by 'mind', may also be paraphrased by the term 'attitude'. An attitude is essentially an internally aroused set of mental-motor predispositions of an individual towards some specific or general stimulus. For this reason it is highly selective and it excludes everything that does not fit into a particular kind of action adopted by the individual. The building up of an attitude is so largely unconscious that often we are not at all aware of how it arises. Sometimes a marginal impression is sufficient to determine the individual's response, because this tangential stimulation touches off and brings to light deep-lying tendencies. This is especially observable in the case-histories of neurotic people, but is also clearly visible in the 'normal' specimens. On the other hand, attitudes may be learned. Education, environmental influences and the many experiences undergone in the course of life, are all active in building an attitude. Whatever may be the origin of a specific attitude, it is essentially the resultant of all the forces operating in life. The most important feature of an attitude, however, is its directionality. Not only does an attitude mark the inception of a response to a certain situation, it also gives direction to the ensuing action. Therefore, it is also characterized by emotionally toned approaches and withdrawals, rejection and acceptance, likes and dislikes. This emotionally toned attitude is known as the 'emotionally toned subjective disposition' (*nyon-mongs-pa'i yid*)[75] and is the basis for the individual's overt activity in the wake of his conceptualizing (intellectually abstracting) activity, which not so much introduces as finalizes the split in his Being, marking the emergence of self-consciousness in which he encounters Being. Since an attitude is both 'intellectual' and 'emotional', it follows that even a 'drive', which we mostly tend to associate with the biological realm, takes on a certain 'meaning'. There are no meaningless drives in the strict sense of the word, hence the division we introduce between drive and spirit is but another instance of the lack of intrinsic awareness. The difficulty we have in understanding of Buddhist and, in particular, Tantric psychology is due to the fact that Buddhism starts from experiential knowledge rather than from a system of concepts or abstract categories as *a priori*. The concern with Being and the potentialities *now* existing implies that what in most philosophies and religions is termed man's 'higher' nature and contrasted with his 'lower' side or, in the specifically Buddhist terminology 'absolute reality' (*paramārthasatya*) and 'commonly accepted reality' (*saṃvṛtisatya*), are both simultaneously defining characteristics of human nature, in the same way as man is both acting and cognizing. When we know fully, suitable action follows automatically and spontaneously. It is significant that 'spontaneity' and 'togetherness' are the possible translations of the Indian word *sahaja*. But when action is divorced from knowledge or knowledge from action, each acts as a powerful fetter, if not as a destructive device. It is their identity that constitutes man's freedom. In the *Vimalakīrtinirdeśasūtra* we read:[76]

> "Action divorced from appreciative discrimination (*prajñā*) is a fetter; appreciative discrimination divorced from action (*upāya*) is a fetter. Action endowed with appreciative discrimination is freedom (*mokṣa*); appreciative discrimination endowed with action is freedom. Their unity, like that of the lamp and its light, is spontaneously understood through the instruction of a competent teacher."

Here we encounter another apparent contrast, that between bondage and freedom. To understand freedom properly we have to start from the basic idea of Tantrism, Being-as-such, and since there can be no other being without nullifying the absoluteness of Being, freedom must be identical with Being-as-such. It is a big irony that Western man who talks so much of freedom should have misunderstood it completely. The fact is that he has defined it either negatively as freedom *from* this or that or compulsively as freedom *to* choose between two pre-ordained entities, according to the dictates of an imaginary super-power. But if freedom and Being-as-such are identical and if it is impossible to have a being other than Being-as-such, what about bondage? The answer is surprisingly simple. Bondage is the result of free activity of the subject taking up an attitude towards the object that is given with him, "neither earlier nor later,' because in 'adopting an attitude towards' we quite literally take up a certain point of view to the exclusion of any other viewpoint and in this way we 'tie ourselves'. Thus, to be, to be aware, to be happy, and to be free are synonyms emphasizing different aspects of one and the same reality.

> "The judicious man who has fully realized his Being as both appreciative discrimination and suitable action, purified from a within and a without, is happy (*sukhita*) in finding no restrictive barriers."[77]

V. Close up of a couple, Nāgārjunakoṇḍa (*Archaeological Survey of India*)

VI. Lumbini Garden, Nāgārjunakoṇḍa (*Archaeological Survey of India*)

In the same way as the status of a sentient being is an alienation from his very Being, emotions are a disruption and fragmentation of ecstatic bliss and of original awareness, which are the two aspects of man's unitary nature and which indicate how the quality of a person's thinking is determined by his feelings and how his feeling is determined by his thinking. Ordinarily we regard thinking as opposed to feeling, because we have tended to restrict thinking to categorical perception and thereby have lost sight of 'existential' thinking which is value-informed perception and which always is 'felt' knowledge. This 'felt' knowledge, before it is intellectually split up into opposing categories such as 'ecstatic bliss' and 'original awareness', represents the functional identity of thinking and feeling grounded in man's existence or Being which, as we have seen, is a dynamic becoming. Being as becoming is technically known as 'appearance' (*snang-ba*), and in its appearance presents itself to itself to be understood as what it is or to be concretized into what it is not but seems to be. In other words, we can view appearance categorically with 'mixed' feelings, or we can view it intrinsically in pure enjoyment. In its intrinsic perception we are set free from the demands our concepts make on what appears, and we can more truly be; or also become more aware of all aspects of reality because our emotional insensitivity is giving way to a heightened feeling of being, and we also can be more natural because the inhibiting and deadening bifurcation into subject and object is dissolved in an original creativity. Padma dkar-po says:[78]

> "Let whatever appears appear, and when in so appearing it is recognized for what it is, all attempts to concretize it (into what it is not), subside by themselves. Thereby, concepts are freed in value-being; emotions are freed in original awareness; and the subject-object division is freed in non-propositional (creativity). This is like ice dissolving in water.
>
> Whatever there is of mental events
> Is of the nature of Lord (Mind-as-such).
> Are the waves different from water?
>
> asks the Great Teacher Saraha. The fact that our concepts

are (i.e., represent and constitute) our value-being, is like the fact that the waves are not different from (their) water."

Padma dkar-po's reference to ice and water[79] shows a deep understanding of human nature. In the symbol of water we easily recognize life pulsating through our body, and to the extent that we feel fully alive we also feel happy, and our joy pervades our environment and enriches everyone who comes into it. However, we all have also met persons who send a chill through us and we speak of them as 'ice-cold', incapable of any emotion. But on closer inspection we will find that a single emotion has usurped their feelings and has made them insensitive to reality.

Just as ice dissolves into its nature, water, so the emotions, 'frozen' fragments of 'felt' knowledge, can be thawed out into original awareness. There is the following 'correspondence' between emotions and awareness:[80]

hostility	. . . . . .	mirror-like awareness
arrogance	. . . . . .	self-sameness awareness
attachment	. . . . . .	distinctness awareness
jealousy	. . . . . .	achievement awareness
infatuation	. . . . . .	Being awareness

Hostility is an emotion that introduces a division where there is none, and its association with perceptual abstraction, the capacity to recognize similarities and, above all, differences among sensible particulars, shows that it thrives in the unremitting cold and bleakness of a frozen wasteland—categorical perception. The thaw will reveal the unitary character of Being, what there really is, like a mirror which in Far Eastern thought is not so much a mechanical reflector, but a powerful means of revealing the true nature of things. The mirror 'reveals' my face whether I like it or not and thus makes me see what I may be reluctant to admit. Rather than presenting fleeting images, it fixes them and makes all other mental operations and kinds of awareness possible.

"The mirror-(like) awareness is stable, the three other
Awarenesses, the awareness of self-sameness, uniqueness,
and achievement, rest on it.
The mirror-(like) awareness is non-subjective, unrestricted,
ever-present,

It is not mistaken about everything knowable and is never biased."[81]

The commentary on these verses emphasizes the unrestricted character of knowledge and awareness, that is, in terms of localization, it cannot be restricted to the sense of self, nor can it be exclusive, while, in terms of temporality, it is not an occasional occurrence, but an ever-present readiness to respond. Furthermore, in order to fulfil its function it must be clear and not shrouded and also must not be tainted by any bias. Indrabhūti even equates this knowledge with absolute Being which then 'mirrors' itself in its awareness:

"Called the All-Good Female, intuited as Mahāmudrā,
This is known as Dharmakāya and also as Mirror-(like) Awareness.
As one's face is seen in a mirror, stable;
So is absolute Being seen in the Mirror-(like)Awareness."[82]

Being-as-such thus confronts itself in the act of self-judgment in the same way as the subject meets himself or herself in the partner, indirectly; the other serves as the subject's mirror:

"Through a mirror one decides (judges) whether one's face is beautiful or ugly; without a mirror one does not see or understand one's face."[83]

But in this act of self-judgment the emerging subjectivism with its ego-centredness distorts the self-image and becomes the emotion of hostility.

Arrogance is the inflated ego. In the paranoid type it develops delusions of grandeur; in the schizoid type it leads to masochistic self-righteousness. The thaw of this over-evaluated selfishness and self-ness, associated with judgments of feeling, leads to an awareness of the self-sameness of 'is-ness'. The individual exists, *is*, simply that; and in the awareness of 'is-ness' he can sense the joy that marks the dissolution of the rigid boundaries between self and other.

Attachment is need-centred 'love', demanding gratification, and for this reason depending on anything or anyone who promises to gratify the need. So one love-supplier is about as good as another. The thaw of this dependence on everything and everyone as a means of having one's needs gratified will lead to an awareness of the intrinsic uniqueness of what is perceived. To see anything and anyone, with all his attributes simultaneously and as necessary to each other, is to give greater validity to perception.

Jealousy is the intolerance of any rival for the possession or attainment of what one regards as peculiarly one's own. It is tied to the attempt of bolstering one's ego and its identification with accomplishments and failures. But ego identifications divert a person from becoming himself. The thaw of ego-centredness shifts attention from the needs of the insatiate ego to the life-sustaining values of Being and leads to an awareness of having achieved or realized what is existentially valuable by having done what is humanly possible.

Infatuation is a response which is quite out of context with a situation because it focuses selectively on one aspect or another and ignores or is oblivious to the rest. It is related to the image we have of our bodily existence but is opposed to the reality of the experience. We experience our world only through our body and the more alive our body is, the more vividly do we perceive our world. But very often our body goes 'dead' (or, more exactly, is made to go dead) as far as its ability to respond to situations is concerned. Fantasies and infatuations then compensate for the loss of awareness. The thaw of infatuation not only restores the aliveness of the body but also leads to an awareness of Being-as-such.

The Way and the Apparent Eroticism of Tantrism

THE attempt to resolve the tension that exists between the feeling of frustration and the sense of fulfilment, between the fictions about man's being and the awareness of his Being, is termed 'the Way'. It is not an inert rod lying between two points, nor is it the favouring of one side in the dilemma that constitutes the human situation, but grounded in Being it is an exercise of regaining and staying with Being. In other words, it is the actualization of intrinsic awareness, Mind-as-such (*sems-nyid*), together with or inseparable from value-being (*chos-kyi-sku*). As this is not the same as the ideas we may have about it, the 'Way' is summarized in the statement:

> "Free from the concepts of *maṇḍala* and (*gaṇa*)*cakra*,
> Of Karmamudrā and Jñānamudrā."[84]

Padma dkap-po explains *maṇḍala* as the 'bearer' (*rten*) of this or that psychic activity, *gaṇa-cakra* (*brten*), manifesting itself as 'divine' forces (*lha*); Karmamudrā as a woman (*mo*) who yields pleasure containing the seed of frustration; and Jñānamudrā as a woman who yields a purer, though unstable, pleasure. He goes on to say:

> "By attending to these facets alone we may be able to reach the Akaniṣṭha realm, the ultimate in sensuousness, but not the absolute, because not free from concretizations, we convert (the real) into un-knowing."[85]

Obviously, our conceptualizations and concretizations of some pleasurable experience may provide a temporary escape, but an escape into sentimentality is not the solution of man's burning problem to find himself. In the same way, an intellectually induced suspension of all mental activity is no answer; nor is the problem solved by an essentially intellectual negativism, as advocated by the Prāsangikas.[86] Sentimentality is compassion divorced from understanding, and the open dimension of Being divorced from all feeling becomes negativism. Therefore Saraha said:

"He who becomes involved with openness without compassion
Will never set forth on the most excellent path.
So also by attending to compassion alone
He will stay in Saṃsāra, but not become free."

Against such one-sided efforts the following statement is directed:

"Do not negate, do not suspend (the mental working), do not find fault,
Do not fix (the mind on something), do not evaluate, but just let be."[87]

In other words, the way is not travelled by abrogating the ability to think, by destroying the inner continuity of one's being and by introducing a division where there is none, but by preserving the unitary character of Being. Again we may quote Saraha:

"He who can combine both (compassion and openness of Being),
Stays neither in Saṃsāra nor in Nirvāṇa."

Moreover, apart from Being there is no other being that can serve as a way:

"Friend, since words falsify, give up this infatuation,
And to whatever you become attached, give that up, too.
Once you understand (the real), all turns out to be It;
Nobody knows anything else but this."

But it is the tendency of our un-knowing to look for our Being where it cannot be. So Saraha declares:

"Where it is present
There we do not see it.
Still, the doctrinaires all explain the texts
But do not understand the Buddha to be in (their) body."

Karma Phrin-las-pa explains this verse as referring to the 'togetherness-awareness' that is present in and with every individual but is not recognized as such by him who is involved with his propositions. Such an individual, therefore, is unable to see Being as it is, but by looking outward he tries to understand what actually is within him. It is in his own body, speech, and mind, that the individual must understand Buddhahood to reside, though not in the manner of the body being a container, but as the representation, the embodiment of Buddhahood. Due to the fact that our concrete existence is an intricate pattern of interacting forces, not only can it be viewed from different angles, but even more so experienced on different levels, and since our individual life is our 'Way', at every step it partakes of ritual and imagery. This can be seen from the following verse by Saraha and its explanation by Karma Phrin-las-pa:

> "By eating and drinking and by enjoying copulation
> Forever and everywhere one fills the rounds.
> Thereby the world beyond is reached,
> And one goes away having crushed the head of infatuation under one's feet."

Karma Phrin-las-pa's interpretation is based on the importance which the tactile sense has for the relationship between man and his outer and inner environment and their corresponding evaluation as well as on the significance of aesthetic perception. We must never forget that man is in the world in the sense that it is through his body that there is for him the corporeality of things, and the interaction between the environment and its impressions on the tactile organs or the body-surface induces sensations of change and intensity in our physical condition. At the same time this experience of materiality and thereby of an objective reality gives way to a visual world picture which is much wider than the limitations imposed by the purely tactile experience, and this is meant by the use of the word 'beyond', which must never be understood as the impossibility of there being a world other than the one we experience. However, there are wide-spread ramifications of the tactile sense, and the corresponding world experiences interlace man with the world or nature on the one hand and with the physiological side of his being on the other. It is this interlacing pattern with various focal points that is termed *rtsa*,[88] which we can best translate by 'pattern', 'structure' and, in specific localizations as 'focal points of experience'.[89] Because of the importance of the tactile sense which gives us immediate contact with the world surrounding us, and because of the fact that we are embodied beings, the cognition that is most highly valued is the aesthetic one, not the one that through its association with concepts introduces the painful separation of object and subject. Togetherness and separateness can best be illustrated by a reference to the place a work of art, particularly sculpture, has in either framework. While the conceptual framework was responsible, as far as our Western tradition is concerned, for removing the work of art from the space and time of our experience and locating it in an ideal space, thereby enabling the spectator to look at it coldly from a distance, in aesthetic perception the work of art remains alive; it calls out to be felt and touched, and each part of it is perceived as if it were for the moment all of the world, unique, desirable, perfect, not needing something other than itself in order to be itself. In this experience there is the warmth of closeness, not the coldness of distance. Instead of disrupting the unity of Being by separating and downgrading the instinctive side, as represented by the tactile experience, from the perceptual side which then becomes over-evaluated conceptually, the Tantric 'Way' attempts to preserve this unity of sensuousness and spirituality, the latter being essentially the former's value, by clarifying the various aspects. It is in this light that Karma Phrin-las-pa gives different interpretations of the above quoted verse by Saraha:[90]

> "Discussing the problem objectively: Having received the (necessary) empowerments,[91] (the person) eats the meat (prepared for) the assemblage and drinks the beer (or other alcoholic beverage). Then he unites with his partner having the appropriate characteristics, by developing three ideas.[92] In the act of the rubbing together of the two organs he concretely fixates and preserves the origination of the four kinds of delight in an ascending or descending manner as taught by the Guru, and thus forever fills the four focal points in his (existential) pattern by making the (*bodhicitta*)

move downward or by forcing it to move upward.[93] By such an experience he reaches a world-transcending Buddhahood experience. Stepping on the head of the worldly people who, not having received the empowerments, are deluded about the maturing effect and, not having received guidance, are deluded about the instruction, one crushes this delusion by (the above) non-delusive method and reaches the level of Buddhahood.

"Discussing the problem in terms of a subjective experience: He who follows the Mantrayoga, eats and drinks the five kinds of nectar in (what is a mixture of) the pure and impure; he unites the motility in (his existential) patterns with the *bodhicitta* and he steadies in his being the awareness of the four kinds of delight due to attending to the process of unification. Continuously attending to this experience he fills the focal points, that is, the pure in his body, with the awareness of absolute bliss. Thereby he attains a Nirvāṇa beyond this world. Stepping on the head of those who are deluded about the Mantrayāna method and crushing this delusion, he goes to a place superior to their status.

"Discussing the problem in terms of a mystical experience: 'Eating' means to know the world of appearance to be mind, through instruction in the meaning of 'memory'; 'drinking' means to know mind to be open, through instruction in the meaning of 'non-memory'; through instruction in the meaning of 'unorigination' appearance and mind meet in one flavour and become united; and through instruction in the meaning of 'transcendence',[94] the self-validating intrinsic awareness rises as spontaneous joy; and by experiencing the ineffable, one forever and everywhere fills one's noetic being with original awareness, through an instruction which is like an uninterruptedly on-going effort; through this experience he goes to the world beyond.

"Discussing the problem from the viewpoint of ultimate Being: A follower of the Mahāmudrā teaching takes as his food the world of appearance rising incessantly in splendour, and has for his drink the open dimension (of Being) merging in the absoluteness of Being. By experiencing the unity and inseparability of appearance and openness of Being he is immediately aware with unsurpassable joy. Forever and everywhere making this experience in the above gradation he fills the rounds, i.e., the world of the knowable or the whole of appearance and possibility, with a spontaneous original awareness, and by this (feeling of) unity he goes to the world beyond."

This fourfold interpretation represents a growing awareness as a continuous process, in which ideas act as functions of unification rather than as separating agents. This, of course, places a different connotation on our concept of ideas which is mainly an instrument for perpetuating the gulf between subject and object and for preventing man from penetrating to his Being which is possible only through experience. According to the above fourfold interpretation, the experience 'A' is understood by the experience 'B', since 'B' is of a higher order than 'A'. To speak, in the last analysis, of an identification of the cognizer with the cognized is another instance of 'misplaced concreteness'. What happens is the emergence of the feeling of unity. The idea as a vehicle of unification is indicated by gNyis-med Avadhūtipa[95] who, in commenting on the first part of Saraha's verse, explains Karma Phrin-las-pa's cryptic 'Three ideas'. They are the idea that the body is a god, speech a mantra, and mind absolute Being. To see the body, by which the body as lived by me is meant, as a god is to appreciate it as a value in its own right; similarly speech as mantra is not empty talk, rather it is communication which does not depend on words with their conventional meaning in usage. Lastly, mind as absolute Being is not the absolutization of subjectivism, it is rather the cognitiveness of Being-as-such which expresses itself in and through the activity of our Mind.

Throughout Tantrism reference is made to the body as lived by me, perceiving, moving, acting, and so on. Taking this reference as our clue we can say that sexuality is itself a mode of being of the person in question, and is concretely interpreted in the stream of lived experience. A human being, whether man or woman, is in this world with his or her body and the body discloses itself as meaningful in its attitudes, gestures, and actions. As an embodied being man is embodied with a certain sex, and the sexuality of the body manifests itself in a variety of manners so that it is justifiable to say that sexuality expresses a human being's existence in the same way as his existence expresses his sexuality. Thus, if the body expresses Existence, it does so because the body actualizes it, and at the same time is its actualization. In other words, the body is not something external to my existence, but is its concrete realization and hence both 'expression' and 'the expressed'. Another point to be noted is that the body discloses itself to my experience as being *mine* and somehow belonging to me who 'lives' it. At the same time it is peculiarly ambiguous, and this ambiguity may be stated as follows: That body over there is simultaneously a woman herself and not herself; her sex presents me with her, and she as embodied presents me with her sex. In the same way, this body here is simultaneously a man himself and not himself; his sex presents her with himself, and he as embodied presents her with his sex. In terms of subject and object, each individual is both subject and object, but the individual is object in a special way, both for himself, as when I speak of *my* body, and for others as a mere body (to be manipulated and controlled). Although human beings are male and female and although sexuality is coextensive with life, sexuality cannot be reduced to Being-as-such, nor can the latter be reduced to sexuality. Hence sexuality is the dialectic of lived experience, in which I apprehend the other as subject or, to put it more cautiously, in which I should apprehend the other as a subject, which means to recognize the intrinsic value of the other, as indicated by the statement that in the realm of lived experience men and women are gods and goddesses.[96] The failure to grasp the meaning of 'Being', of 'body'and 'sexuality' has resulted in a thorough misunderstanding of Buddhist Tantrism. This is mainly due to the difference of 'climate' contributing to the development of ideas. Western civilization derives from the early Mediterranean slave societies with their attendant postulate of a celestial lawgiver who 'legislates' for both human beings and non-human natural phenomena, and who 'owns' the human beings as his chattels, just as a shepherd owns his flock and takes up an active attitude of command. Pastoral dominance, on the one hand, and among seafaring people, the unquestioning obedience to the one in command of a ship, on the other, greatly assisted the development of a 'dominance' psychology which attempts to rationalize the crave for power, domination, and control. It aims not only at turning the other into an object to be used or misused at will, but also at making the other feel as an object in the eyes of the master or postulated super-power. This is, of course, impossible because an object, a slave, cannot give the recognition sought for by the master as only a subject can do so, and it is precisely the individual's subject character that the master cannot tolerate and that he attempts to deny. Inasmuch as Hindu Tantrism has been deeply influenced by the dominance psychology of the Sāṃkhya system, professing a dualism of *puruṣa* who is male, and of *prakṛti* who is female and who dances or stops dancing at the bidding of the Lord or *puruṣa*, this purely Hinduistic power mentality, so similar to the Western dominance psychology, was generalized and applied to all forms of Tantrism by writers who did not see or, due to their being steeped so much in dominance psychology, could not understand that the desire to realize Being is not the same as the craving for power. Hence Tantrism was equated with 'power'. And since *puruṣa* and *prakṛti* involved a sexual symbolism, which was concretized in the sense that the sexual act was the proof of one's masculinity, the paranoid Western conception about Tantrism resulted: it is the paranoid who is obsessed with his sexual potency and attempts to compel the object to come towards him (the *prakṛti* dances at the bidding of the *puruṣa*). He tries to make the other (*the* woman) responsible for the action of satisfying his needs. At the same time he identifies himself with his sexuality, and this identification becomes the basis for his idea of power, preferably of 'omnipotence'.

It is a fact that any dominance psychology inevitably destroys the individual as subject. Its dehumanizing force was keenly felt by those brought up in the Western world and so they turned to the 'mysterious' East which was supposed to hold the key to their acquiring the powers that the Western institutions denied them. But exchange of one kind of dominance for another does not lead to the realization of Being; it remains a slave's dream of becoming a master.

There is another area in which the destruction of the individual as a living being is deeply felt, and where traditional Western religion fails and has always failed us. This is the feeling of sex, rigorously excluded from the realm of speech and thought and frowned upon in deeds. This exclusion, too, has a long history and is inextricably tied up with the contempt for and fear of the body. The official attitude has been and is in favour of continence, abstinence and asceticism having their root in fear, and while contempt might assist the official attitude, it more often has been in opposition to it, particularly in its aspect of defiance. Libertinism did not appear under the auspices of communion and joy, but under those of arrogance and contempt. To suffer from an obsessive fear of the body is perhaps not so different from a compulsive addiction to sex, be these addicts virility-provers or seductiveness-provers. The important point to note is that in all these cases sex is confined to only one dimension, sensual pleasure and exploitation, but the aesthetic experience of joy and through it the enrichment of one's Being is missed. The use of sex as an instrument of power distorts its function. Instead of being an experience of feeling for the partner, it becomes a manoeuvre to establish one's imaginary superiority. A man who sees himself as a sexual object will imagine himself as 'the great lover', and a woman who sees herself as a sexual object believes in the irresistibility of her sex appeal. Both may feel repelled by their body, but they are convinced of its power.

Tantrism certainly is not on the side of asceticism, but it would be wrong to conclude that therefore it must of necessity advocate libertinism and that its appeal to Western man, reared in an atmosphere hostile to women, pleasure, and life, is due to the fact that Tantrism approves of women and of sex and, by implication, can serve as the moral justification for the sex addict's compulsion. It is true, Tantrism recognizes pleasure as valuable and positive, but much more than mere pleasure-seeking is involved. It is equally true that in its Hinduistic form it combines power with pleasure which essentially is appreciation and is meant to lead to aesthetic enjoyment, and so has a positive content, unlike Christianity which advocates the impotence of man, denounces pleasure and condemns its source, woman.[97] Buddhist Tantrism dispenses with the idea of power, in which it sees a remnant of subjectivistic philosophy, and even goes beyond mere pleasure to the enjoyment of being and of enlightenment unattainable without woman.

"How can enlightenment be attained in this bodily existence
Without thine incessant love, o lovely young girl?"[98]

Enlightenment is the name for a change in perspective, and Tantrism is the practical way of bringing about this change. It does not mean that in this change of perspective something is seen that others cannot see, but that things and, above all, persons are seen differently. This is clearly stated by Padma dkar-po:[99]

> "In attending to the vision of (seeing himself as) a god (*lha*) the yogi apprehends, not incorrectly, what ordinarily appears before his eyes; however, mentally he takes a firm pride in his being a god (*lha'i sku*). This is termed *adhiṣṭhānayoga*. In this term, *adhi* means 'superior', and *ṣṭhāna* means 'arrangement', 'accomplishment', 'adornment', hence 'to be graced'. A 'superior accomplishment' is termed 'superior feeling of reverence' from the root *adhimuñc*."

To see oneself as a god is to be aware of one's existence as valuable and as good; it is not deifying one's shortcomings which are the products of a limited and selfish vision and hence negative and evil. The emotional quality of this value-perception is the 'feeling of reverence' which is not contradictory to exaltation or pride; the negative counterpart to pride is arrogance and to reverence, contempt and self-debasement. The attempt to see oneself as a god is not yet to be enlightened, but it enfeebles the negative view one takes of oneself.[100] Only by taking a positive view of oneself can one truly be. The experience of really being is not only felt as blissful but is also an identity-experience.

Here man has found himself and is no longer a 'thing-of-and-in-the-world'. In order to find himself man needs the 'other' who is no intellectual abstraction, but part of himself, needed in order to be himself. Sahajayoginī Cintā, speaking of the state when one spontaneously is oneself, says:[101]

> "Here, in spontaneity which is non-dual and naturally pure, one's Being (*bdag-nyid*), in order that one may understand one's Being, manifests itself in the shape of man and woman."

The concrete 'other' person, for me, is whoever enters my life-world and whom I accept as one accepting me in order to accept me or her as one who is willing to accept me as one accepting myself. This complex situation of the interaction of man and woman is termed Karmamudrā and Jñānamudrā, the one referring to the 'without', the other to the 'within', each of them representing an 'encounter' that changes both partners.

A. Karmamudrā—an 'outward' encounter.

According to Nāropa, who briefly refers to the charms of woman elaborated in Indian ornate poetry:[102]

> "Karmamudrā means a woman with firm breasts and a rich display of hair. She is the impetus and sustaining power of pleasure in the realm of desire (Kāmadhātu). Karma implies kissing, embracing, touching of the private parts, erection of the penis, and so on and so forth. A *mudrā* which is characterized by initiating these occurrences is said to set up a certain relationship. This relationship yields only a self-defeating pleasure. The term *mudrā* itself is used, because (such a woman) gives joy (*mudaṃ*) and sexual gratification (*ratiṃ*)."

It is in the realm of the sex drive and in the fever of desire that, to all outward appearance, the relationship between man and woman expresses itself most effectively. But although all drives postulate and even enforce fulfilment with reference to their objective, they cannot be evaluated as to their biological domain exclusively. Such could only be the case if man and woman were totally unaware of themselves as well as of each other. Yet each is aware of his sex, while the tendencies and features of the other sex appear 'extrajected' and give rise to a longing for the other sex. This results in a rather fanciful perception of reality, because wherever a subject establishes a rapport with an object, there will occur projections and objectivations. Projection is either subject-related or object-related. In the former case, qualities of an extraject, that is, object representations which emerge in extra-jection, are incorrectly imputed to an external object; in the latter case, qualities of an object remembered are incorrectly imputed to an external object. These two factors determine what one 'sees' in the other. Actually, one encounters oneself in the other who, in turn, encounters himself or herself in myself, because between subject and object, myself and the other, there exists the relationship of reactivity. The less an individual is aware of his Being and the more he is concerned with what he believes himself to be, the more he comes under the spell of the fictions of his own making, and the more he becomes entangled in the so-called 'objective' world, where he believes that he can find what he wants and needs, the farther he is led away from himself. The dependence on the object, the woman, will not appear to him as dependence. By having intercourse with the woman and by becoming absorbed in the spell of the sex drive he may have the feeling that his insularity has been abolished and that he has been reunited with what was wanting in him. However, only an extremely fragile solution has been found. Plagued by frustration and haunted by anxiety, he is tempted into the vicious circle of seeking all the more in the objective world around him, in order to quench the burning thirst and to still the gnawing hunger for total satisfaction.

What happens may be gleaned from the 'four momentary situations' and 'four intensities of joy' in connection with the Karmamudrā. The first, 'variedness', comprises both the stimulus of the object and the attention given by the subject. Its feeling correlate is joy. The second, 'maturation' or 'elaborated response', is the process that combines the various stimuli into a fairly coherent whole. The feeling correlate is transport. The third, 'climax', is related to the feeling of spontaneity, 'to-be-wholly-

VII. A couple, Nāgārjunakoṇḍa (*Archaeological Survey of India*)

VIII. A couple, Nāgārjunakoṇḍa (*Archaeological Survey of India*)

with'. But it generally gives way to a 'break-down' and the feeling of quiescence. In more concrete terms, first a man and a woman become attracted to and interested in each other. The man then 'explores' the charms of his partner, his exploration in the end leading to intercourse. With the orgasm the climax is reached. He now believes himself to be 'existentially aware', but his knowledge breaks in his hands, and he has to start all over again. The climax, expected to come from outside, cannot fulfil the expectations because it is based on a postulate, and so the climax becomes man's very failure which, due to the inherent unknowing, becomes responsible for the exaggeration of sex behaviour, for nymphomania in the female and satyrism in the male, and for the peculiar attitudes of those who have been taught that sex is the most base activity of man, all of a sudden discovering that it is the most basic one and that there is nothing else.

The unmistakably erotic language must not deceive us. As embodied beings we use symbols derived from the phenomenal world and from fundamental, human experience. Man's sexuality is but one among the many 'expressions' of his Being and of what is 'expressed' in the body which is mind as well. As a term for an impressive encounter, the Karmamudrā is more a symbol than a sign and does not exclusively point to the woman of the physical world, but to occurrences of which the woman herself and the encounter with her are a symbol. Therefore it is not so much a matter of what one does with her, but of how it feels to be with her.

> "The way of the Karmamudrā is to feel the awareness of the sixteen kinds of intensities of joy when after having properly united with her one's creative energy is released from the 'head' and descends to the tip of the 'jewel',"

says Padma dkar-po,[103] who here refers to the perception of pleasure as a rhythmic and pulsatory activity of the body.

More explicit is Karma Phrin-las-pa commenting on a verse by Saraha, which according to gNyis-med Avadhūtipa refers to the Karmamudrā as such. Saraha's words are:

> "Where motility and intentionality are not operative
> And where neither sun nor moon appear,

There, you fools, let mind relax restfully.
Having given all the instructions Saraha has gone away."

Karma Phrin-las-pa gives various interpretations, all of them related to the sensations experienced in the body-schema:[104]

"Explaining this verse literally; When you have the experience (of the Karmamudrā), let the mind relax and rest there, where the motility of the concepts and the intentions of memory and perception do not operate and where the concepts (through which) one sees mind's activity symbolized by sun and moon[105] like an apparition, do not enter. (With the word 'let') Saraha addresses those who do not know (the meaning of) existential presence and, having given them all instructions, he has gone away.

"Explaining this verse in a general context; The symbol of motility indicates movement and refers to the 'seventh (emotionally predisposed, ego-centred) mind'; the symbol of intentionality indicates the intention of the 'sixth (or categorically perceptive) mind'.[106] When the concepts of subject and object deriving from these (two 'minds') are not operative and when the concretization of 'appearance' symbolized by the sun and the concretization of 'openness' symbolized by the moon, and the addictiveness deriving from them does not occur, one relaxes in a state of self-sameness (i.e. identity-experience).

"Explaining this verse as to its hidden meaning: When one experiences the way of desire[107] and when motility which is the vehicle of conscious perception, and the intentionality of perception are not operative, the idea of 'object' fades away since the sun-motility to the right (of the body-schema) is not active and so does the idea of 'subject' since the moon-motility to the left (of the body-schema) is not active. Relax then in the centre where subject and object do not prevail.

"Explaining this verse from the viewpoint of ultimate Being: When a person through the four *mudrās*[108] which are the specific methods in the Mantrayāna, realizes his goal, the motility of the four elementary forces (rigidity, cohesion, temperature, movement) ceases and turns into the motility of pure awareness; so also the intentionality moving in the subject-object dichotomy ceases to operate and, free from all concrete indications and concrete feelings, it becomes the centre where internally sun and moon do not shine. Relax in this state which brings forth the three Indestructibles (of authentic being, communication, and responsiveness). With these words Saraha or (any other competent) Guru gives instruction to those who do not know the appropriate methods."

Although the language is highly technical, the message is clear. The symbol of the Karmamudrā points not from the sensuous and aesthetic experience of her to her being a physical- chemical-electromagnetic-biological body indirectly verified by postulates, but from one factor in this aesthetic experience to another. Abstract concepts give way to emotionally moving images. In other words, the aesthetically immediate, present in the inter-subjective relationship between man and woman, is not used as the springboard for arriving at postulationally perceived, indirectly verified beliefs about three-dimensional, external objects, and what the subject then can do with or to them, but is appreciated in its own right. In the case of the Karmamudrā as a stimulating situation, sexuality is a value in the sense that it is the manifestation in determinate, transitory, and limited form of absolutely real and irreducible Being. But like all manifestations it is ambiguous; it can lead man to himself as much as it can destroy his humanity. If and to the extent that in the Karmamudrā situation the partners enjoy a strong sense of affinity and harmonious complementariness, their action leads to the deepest possible experience of Being; but if and to the extent that the partners feel alienated or estranged, they will merely create an illusion that perpetuates their alienated condition. *He* will try to prove himself to be the 'perfect lover' and in this attempt will be only pre-occupied with his ego image. *She* will try to prove herself to be the 'perfect wife' or 'love goddess' and become insensitive to her husband's feelings. Both partners who seemingly live for nothing but the sensations the sexual act may afford, are incapable of enjoying their partnership and merely go through the motions of being together.

B. Jñānamudrā—an 'inward' encounter.

While the Karmamudrā is basically the encounter with a physical woman, which in the context of the physiological realm gives only a self-defeating pleasure (*omne animal post coitum triste*), the Jñānamudrā is "the imaginary personification of the aesthetically appreciative and discriminative perceptive function, and lets one taste some fleeting bliss through appearing radiantly in concentration."[109] More explicit is the description by Nāropa:[110]

> "Jñānamudrā is the creation of one's own mind. She is of the nature of the Great Mother[111] or other goddesses and comprises all that has been previously experienced. She is the impetus and sustaining power of pleasure in the realm of aesthetic forms (Rūpadhātu). The awareness (of her) is marked by reminiscences of former experiences such as smiles and enjoyments. This relationship yields satiety."

Two points have to be clarified lest they lead to a serious misunderstanding of what is meant by the Jñānamudrā. The one is the statement that 'she' is a creation of one's mind. Somehow the word 'creation' evokes in us the idea of a product, and we tend to overlook the actual creativeness that becomes formulated in what we prosaically call a product. Creativeness is the characteristic of mind and is its special kind of perceptiveness that can see anew and afresh and therefore lives far more in the world of the real than in the world of concepts and other stereotypes with which most people confuse the real. The other is the statement that 'she' is a personification of the aesthetically perceptive function and by nature a goddess. Personification is a term that originated in the animistic theory that attempted to 'explain' primitive conscious life according to the fallacies of Anglo-French positivism. The Jñānamudrā experience does not wish to 'explain' anything, it records how the experience comes to a man in visible and intelligible forms. To call the function a goddess, and, by transference, to say that woman is a goddess incarnate may be poetry. But poetry does not tell lies; it means what it says, but it does not always say all that it means. Poetry, like any other art, is a special revelation of the reality whose nature is determined by an awareness of value and its appreciation. The symbolic expressions of the poet are his means of apprehending and expressing values otherwise not expressible. Their appraisal and appreciation involve the feelings because values, unless they are arbitrarily assigned values, are not intellectually and conceptually detachable from the real. Through the goddess man gains a living vision of reality. To see in the woman a goddess is not simply a sentimentality, it rather indicates the uniqueness of such an experience and its content is inexpressible by any other category. Man and goddess are two forms or moulds in which Being expresses itself. The goddess is not merely a flight of fancy, and man is not an abject thing-in-the-world. The relationship between the two is rather like the one between the participants in a ballet. In the interplay between man and goddess one has the feeling of how wonderfully the divine part is enacted and how real man is, but also of how unsuspecting each is of the other. When the one moves, a complementary movement is seen in the other. When man turns altogether too human, the goddess threatens him; when he unassumingly turns to her she lovingly goes near him. Then suddenly the tableau changes. The man submits to the world of the divine and the goddess displays her beauty in the world of man. The former partnership founded on expectations becomes a partnership grounded in values perceived. The goddess here becomes a bridge between man and his Being.

Such a vision is not a mere abstraction, but is a tangibly perceived and felt situation, as Padma dkar-po points out:[112]

> "The way of the Jñānamudrā is to become firmly habituated to (a vision of greater reality) by purifying all that is subsumed under the psycho-physical constituents, the elementary forces, and the interactional fields, through the image of a god; then when one has the experience of properly feeling and seeing the *maṇḍala*,[113] one unites with Vajravarāhī or Nairātmyā or any other goddess, being the formulation of the aesthetically appropriate function, and through this union the fire of original awareness blazes

> forth, and one's creative energy, melted by this fire, flows to the Vajra and the centre of the Padma and all the senses and their objects settle in the sixteen kinds of joy having the same flavour in absolute bliss."

It is significant that in this experience reference is made to the creative energy which is allowed to flow freely, just as in the description of the Karmamudrā. The difference is that the Jñānamudrā experience makes man see his biological background of his life in a different light. 'She' becomes a balm to the mind divided against itself by the conflict of concepts. 'She' is then an education in loving and an adventure in fulfilment, a search for higher integration:

> "Highest mistress of the world!
> Let me in the azure
> Tent of Heaven, in light unfurled
> Hear thy Mystery measure!
> Justify sweet thoughts that move
> Breast of man to meet thee!
> And with holy bliss of love
> Bear him up to greet thee!"

says the German poet Goethe and, unsuspectingly, voices the Buddhist awareness of the Jñānamudrā.

Through the goddess man is enabled to see more of himself and his Being and also comes closer to his Being by seeking out through love what is real and unique, for the goddess is 'aesthetically appreciative-discriminative perceptiveness' (*shes-rab-ma*) which singles out the real from the fictitious, in short, 'value-cognition'. Such cognition helps us to remove the obstacles which by un-knowing we put up between ourselves and life. Although we often say that love is blind, it would be more correct to recognize the fact that love is more perceptive and ready to accept what has been repressed or spurned for 'moral' or other rationalizations. When love prevails, the individual is no longer preoccupied with the hate-and-contempt inspired attempts to change things (or persons) that enter his life by reforming, punishing them, protecting himself against their alleged interference, either by forestalling or by crushing them. The whole net of intriguing concepts that intervene between himself and the other and make the recognition of his Being through the respect for the other who is part of this Being impossible, vanishes. Love heals the wounds of separateness and gives dignity to what there is. Through it the worlds are not annihilated, but shine in a more beautiful light. Therefore, according to gNyis-med Avadhūtipa, Saraha's words:

"Do not create duality, create unity!
Without setting up distinctions between the patterns,
Colour the whole triple world
In absolute love colour and . . ."

refer to the Jñānamudrā experience.[114]

While the Karmamudrā, manipulating organs, unless it merely employs sex to prove prowess and sensuality to hide sensitivity, can lead to and causally initiate the Jñānamudrā, making love, and while the latter brings us closer to our Being, it is not the same as Being, and also cannot causally initiate Being. Rather, Being is presupposed by the Karmamudrā and the Jñānamudrā through which we as embodied beings catch a glimpse of our Being. Therefore also, even love, Jñānamudrā, gives us merely a fleeting sense of bliss, although this feeling is of a higher, and hence more positive, order than the Karmamudrā who makes us 'sad' in the pleasurable feeling she provides ("it's so quickly over").

Being-as-such cannot be reduced to an object and every attempt to objectify it destroys its life-sustaining reality. Nor can it be equated with a self or subject, which is the organizing function of an individual by means of which one human being relates himself to another. And yet in the experience of Being-as-such we experience ourselves as being most ourselves without creating a 'self' that introduces a rift into our Being. While we can *be*, we cannot describe it, and only from the periphery, as it were, can we point to it and illustrate it by referring to instances in which we experience Being most poignantly, as when we have a sudden insight after having struggled in vain for days. The experience is so overwhelming that it makes us want to express it, but words fail us. Being impresses itself on us in such a way that we may refer to it as an encounter in an absolute sense, Mahāmudrā, but in the end we have to concede with Saraha:

> "There is neither beginning, middle, nor end;
> It is neither Saṃsāra, nor Nirvāṇa!
> As to this supreme and absolute bliss
> 'Tis neither a self nor another."[115]

The fact that we are able, though rarely, to be aware without the intervention of our prejudices and concepts, to love without making demands, and to be without playing a role, gives us a basis of meaning for our embodied existence and our actions. This basis is referred to by the technical term Samāyāmudrā, the commitment to be.

Thus we have four encounters with Being (*mudrā*)[116] which are related in a specific way. We begin with the Karmamudrā and, if we are lucky, i.e., healthy, proceed through her to the Jñānamudrā through whom we are enabled to realize our Being, or Mahāmudrā, which informs us as embodied beings through the Samāyāmudrā. In other words, we begin with sex which quite literally is the beginning of ourselves, but sex is not a mere manipulation of organs; it generates an awareness which may turn into undemanding love, and it is through such love that we see the world and ourselves in a different light, and develop an unclouded awareness of the value of being. What on the previous level was a cold abstraction becomes now a living symbol pointing to the source, Being-as-such, and through its experience we return to the world differently. Thus Maitripa says:[117]

> "Karmamudrā is the awareness that comes from a woman with firm breasts and a rich display of hair, who has learned her part well; the Dharmamudrā or Jñānamudrā is an attention by sealing all that is engendered in the union with such a Karmamudrā, or it is an attention by not becoming separated from an awareness that (knows that) all that is is like an apparition by having investigated it by the syllogism of the one and the many. Mahāmudrā is the integrated state of the radiant light. Samāyāmudrā is to act for ever on behalf of the sentient beings through the two Rūpakāyas out of the sphere of this radiant light."

Being in the world again, but differently, carries with it the feeling of certainty; the individual feels himself to be his own master, free from doubts, no longer haunted by questions whose answers elude him. Less a thing-of-the-world, the person has become the embodiment of values and radiates these values which become discernible to the observer. This is the meaning of acting on behalf of others through the Rūpakāyas, which are both inwardly felt and outwardly observed and can be described both ways, and which have their root in the 'radiant light', which is not some mysterious entity but the radiance of an alive person.

Saraha is again our guide here. He says:

> "In front and in the rear and in the ten directions
> Whatever one sees is It;
> Of this day, a master,[118] I have destroyed error:
> Now I need not ask anyone."

Symbols of Unity and Transformation

SINCE Tantrism aims at bringing man closer to his Being, it employs many methods of which the sex experience is only one. Because of this fact Tantrism is not a philosophy of sex. However, due to the fact that it recognizes sex as a powerful means of bringing about a change in perspective, much misunderstanding has resulted. It is true that the sexual organs are a natural focus of both sensation and interest in erotic experience, but it is not so much the physiological aspect with which Tantrism is concerned, but the experience itself and the effect it has on the individual. Somehow, in the course of history, Western man has been led astray by his economic and biological model so that he can hardly think of sex as anything else but the gratification of a physiological need. Consequently the subtler distinction that Tantrism makes between the physiological side and its 'symbolical' meaning is overlooked and reduced to the 'nothing but'. Another source of misunderstanding is the naive belief that words have meanings and, in this particular case, only one meaning. The fact is that words are sounds that acquire or are assigned meanings by usage and in this process those who use words do one of two things: either they report what people in general, using the language they speak, already mean by it, or they stipulate a use and meaning; that is, they state what they are going to mean by it. Stipulating a meaning is most often the result of a moving experience and, since more often than not, words already available in a given language are used for stipulative definitions, it seems that the word used indicates a certain resemblance or analogy that is felt to exist between the experience referred to by the word and the inexpressible, non-conceptualizable X which the word or symbol is said to stand for. This distinction between reportive terms and stipulative terms is clearly observed in the two cases of Karmamudrā and Jñānamudrā. For us as embodied beings it is only natural that we first start with our body and its organs (note the impersonal diction as if the body were something alien to us), and with how we manage and manipulate them. Hence the Karmamudrā is aptly reported to initiate embraces, kisses, touching the erogenous zones and finally the climax in the act of copulation.

"In uniting with the Karmamudrā and in making love to the Jñānamudrā
The *bodhicitta*, quintessence of bliss, has to be preserved, by those of firm vows.
Having inserted the prick in the cleft he may not let go the *bodhicitta*,
But must attend to the Buddha-vision, encompassing the three worlds."[119]

Although at first glance this statement may seem to refer to the moment of penetration and little else, the associations that go with the words used in the original, point to something much more important. The same text explains:

"Cleavage is called cleft because it rends apart the deadening power of the conflicting emotions;
The conflicting emotions are to be overcome by value-cognition, therefore value-cognition is called the cleft."[120]

This shows that even the Karmamudrā is never a matter of mere physiological sex, a preoccupation with the orgasm, but that the situation summed up by the term Karmamudrā engenders an awareness of ever-new facets of the experience. The awareness thus engendered is a 'transcendent function' (*pāramitā*), as it releases the individual from his thing-related concern and opens him to an appreciation of the value of Being, but does not annihilate him in a nihilistic transcendentalism. Therefore Anangavajra says:[121]

"(As) the transcendent function of discriminative-appreciative awareness she has to be served by those desirous of liberation,

Pure in her absoluteness, only in this empirical world has she assumed the shape of a woman.
In the shape of a woman she is everywhere present.
Therefore the Vajranātha has said that she comes from the outer world."[122]

In the following description of her he grows quite lyrical:

"Like a ship sailing to its peaceful harbour, she saves all beings,
From the terrible ocean of birth, surging with waves of old age.
Divine, beautiful, rich in qualities, she quickly leads to realization,
Like the Wish-Fulfilling Gem she provides whatever one desires.
Without her, who is praised by Vajradhara, and who is the quintessence of all Buddha qualities,
No realization is possible; therefore those desirous of liberation should wisely follow her unrivalled conduct.
By following her whose lotus-feet have been worshipped by Murāri, Indra, Śiva, Kubera, Brahma, and others,
And her evil-destroying course, the Tathāgatas have reached the highest state."[123]

It is through the development of the appreciative and discriminative function that man is led out of the world of biological desires, where he is driven on to seek a satisfying release and pleasurable relief, to a world of enjoyment and appreciation. It is the same world, but experienced differently. Its perception has been given major scope, depth, and dignity. It differs from ordinary perception which is merely a means to a metaperceptual end, and is reduced to a very economical recording of qualities and events significant for these ends; in other words, in the Karmamudrā situation I take stock of the woman's vital statistics and what they may offer for gratification. But even here flickers of aesthetic experiences occur, although they are mostly incidental. But in the Jñānamudrā situation the opposite is the case. Whatever is perceived is done to serve perception, to make it more clear and precise, more ample and subtle. Within the orbit of such perception, as here understood, sensation, feeling, imagination, preferences, and interests operate as much as the physiological factors. But the main point is that in such a perception the total being of the participant is brought into action. Thus Anangavajra says:[124]

"Soon after he has embraced his mudrā, and started to insert the sceptre,
To drink from her nectar-moist lips, to induce her to speak cooingly,
To enjoy rich delights, and to make her thighs quiver,
King Cupid, Vajrasattva, will certainly be realized."

The bodily description can hardly be more realistic and yet the situation has changed, and the language (in the original) expresses it. Here, sceptre (*vajra*) and, by implication, lotus (*padma*), are the indicators. Unlike the corresponding terms of the Karmamudrā situation, *linga* and *bhaga*, these terms connotate an emotionally changed value. By 'sceptre' or, more literally, 'diamond', is meant what is undestructible and the primary factor in the nature of things, and what is felt to be valuable and a solid basis for one's being. Its definition runs as follows:[125]

"It is firm, round, cannot be changed, be pierced, be split,
Cannot be burnt, is indestructible and (as) openness (*śūnyatā*) it is called *vajra*."

In the term Vajrasattva, which refers to the change that has been effected, when, so to speak, we have been enabled to love instead of temporarily 'falling in and out of love', *vajra* indicates the bliss that is experienced when authentic being, communication and responsiveness have become an integrated whole, while the term *sattva* refers to the world as cognized integratively. The unity, as expressed in the symbol Vajrasattva, is not so much a placing of the experience in a system of concepts or even words but a savouring of the qualities of the experience, particularly of that which cannot be put into words or reduced to something other than itself. This is technically known as *śūnyatā*, a term that has been grossly misunderstood, as its translation by 'empty' and 'void' indicates. *Śūnyatā* is a term for the absolutely positive. It is nothing, when compared with what ordinary perception is about, but as an utter openness it is an infinite source of what we can only inadequately indicate by a feeling of perfection, completeness, freedom. But in order to perceive this openness perception itself must be open and untainted, not internally warped by any bias. In other words, it must be perceptive, appreciative, not forceful, demanding. Rather than trying to change the experience and make it something other than it is, it submits and surrenders to the experience. This is done by the *prajñā*, an appreciative-discriminative function, perceptive of values that cannot be shorn away from the reality of Being. While *vajra* is a symbol for the ultimate and indestructible quality of Being, which is the same as being aware, the suppleness of this appreciative awareness is indicated by the symbol of the lotus flower (*padma*). Since early times the lotus flower has been a symbol of creativity producing the world of things from its fertile seeds, and of purity, because water does not cling to its leaves. This symbol is used by Saraha in describing the peak-experience of Being which is *in this* world, but not just this world:

> "Even when among the objects and pressed hard by the desire for them—
> —As long as he has not this spontaneity, he clings to evil—
> He is not affected by the objects enjoying them,
> Just as water does not cling to the leaves of a lotus flower."

gNyis-med Avadhūtipa elaborates as follows:[126]

> "The external objects are the five pleasurable sense-perceptions, the internal objects are 'memory'. Indulging in them, but not being aware of the real, a person imagines them as an assembly of gods and goddesses, both in the within and in the without. (This is meant by Saraha when he says): 'Even when among the objects and pressed hard by the desire for them . . .' However, spontaneity as a god is not a creation of the mind; only a (mind-created) god is unhealthy. (Hence Saraha states): 'As long as he has not this spontaneity, he clings to evil.'—The ground of all that is is the spontaneity that is not a creation of the mind. If one is aware of this—'He is not affected by the objects when enjoying them.' To give an example: a blue or white

lotus flower or jasmine-flower can enthrall a person with its lovely colour, its softness and its fragrance. That it can do so lies in the fact that it grows in the unclean ponds of villages and hamlets, but is not affected by their uncleanliness. The same holds good for the attitude of the yogi. Even if he 'thinks' of the objects of the outer and inner world, by knowing the real, he is not affected by the mire of the objects and taking the lotus flower without its (surrounding) mire, he understands the absolutely real without its (deflecting) ideas."

The imagery and symbolism clearly point to the aesthetic experience which in connection with the Jñānamudrā is freed from the narrowness of the specific practical dealing with the Karmamudrā. The aesthetic experience, however, is not exhausted by being a valuable addition to the other moments of our lived existence, it also possesses instrumental values. It can be a means of self-growth by enlarging the horizon of meaning and by diminishing the tendencies to seize and exploit. Nonetheless, the aesthetic experience is not an end in itself, it is a stimulation to the one who has the experience. As far as the 'object matter' is concerned, there is no difference between ordinary and aesthetic perception; but while ordinary perception is inhibitive and restricted to an immediate purpose, aesthetic perception sets the observer free by letting all that is present in the object appear in the fullest and most vivid manner, thus enabling a more lively appreciation of the actualities of the object and preventing a distortion of the object by the imposition of subjective fancy. This is meant by the statement that a person becomes free in intrinsic perception. That aesthetic perception is not an end, although it is superior to ordinary perception, is stated by Saraha, contrasting the Karmamudrā and Jñānamudrā:

"In coition to find bliss supreme
Without knowing the real, is like
A thirsty man who pursues a mirage: will he ever
Find the heavenly nectar before he dies of thirst?
Ineffective is the revelling
In that most blissful feeling

Which lies between the Padma and the Vajra;
How will he fulfill the hopes of the three worlds?"[127]

In a more prosaic way we can restate Saraha's words as follows: Karmamudrā as an end sums up the frustrating efforts of the pleasure-chaser, the compulsive collector of physical contacts; Jñānamudrā as an end is an aestheticistic mood which tends to make the individual being out of touch with the situation. Karmamudrā is the situation in which a man finds himself, who seeks fun and is 'in for kicks', while pleasure eludes him; Jñānamudrā is the situation of the drug addict who changes his inner reality, but does nothing, and is utterly incapable of doing anything, about the depressiveness and grimness of the external situation.

One other point must be noted in this connection which is significant for Tantric thought. Ordinary perception is ego-centred, harsh, aggressive, imposing; aesthetic perception is object-centred, receptive, appreciative. In it the object becomes the guide, and the subject submits to its lead. This submissive union of the subject with the object, an aesthetic union, is undertaken for a more intimate appreciation of the object's intrinsic value and being which is, paradoxically, the subject's very being. Here subject and object become identical in nature. Kāṇha says:[128]

"In the same way as salt dissolves in water, so also the mind embraced by his spouse
Goes to identity of feeling (*samarasa*) the very moment it remains with her."

Kāṇha's words, read in connection with the statement that in the aesthetic experience of the Jñānamudrā the woman is seen as a goddess, reveal a very important point. In the aesthetic union the subject is transformed in terms of the object, because only by becoming a god himself is the subject able to perceive the goddess. In other words, to the extent that we are more 'ourselves' we can be aware of the other as more 'himself' or 'herself'. This experience is not of something other than what there is, but is a very intensive existential awareness. On the other hand, to imagine a god or goddess as over and above or outside the

IX. A couple, Nāgārjunakoṇḍa (*Archaeological Survey of India*)

X. Vajradhara (rDo-rje-'chang): Symbol of the Absolute in its polarity aspect (*Author's collection*)

experience and to conceive of Him or Her as the ground of Being, is to absolutize a fiction and the negation of the absoluteness of Being. There cannot be any 'other' being but Being-as-such without invalidating Being-as-such, hence there cannot be any 'other' god or goddess over and against Being-as-such. It is the mistake of all theisms (monotheism, polytheism, pantheism and so on) to invent a god in order to conceal their existential incompetence and to escape from existential responsibility. Responsibility means to *respond* in the *knowledge* that the world around me is glowingly *alive*, not to cling to beliefs which without exception are based on a distortion, if not a flat denial, of reality and which constitute no value at all. When the quest for knowledge is sin and ignorance a virtue, no responsibility is possible, and as Saraha and gNyis-med Avadhūtipa point out, an invented god is evil and mentally unhealthy. The historical record of all theistic religions provides all the necessary evidence for Saraha's indictment.

Because of its intrinsically 'divine' character the aesthetic experience is of greatest importance as a preparation for the creation of works of art. We have only to think of the vast number of sculptures and paintings of Buddhist 'deities' (actually a misnomer as they are representations of aspects of Buddhahood), who have taken from the physical environment the suggestions for their sensuous execution. Their aim is to transform their creators and beholders into intrinsically satisfied perceptual agents, satisfied because they have come closer to their Being. The relationship that Tantrism has to the development of the fine arts shows that it is not merely a sex preoccupation, the pastime of the modern West's 'hollow men'.

Karmamudrā and Jñānamudrā are, on an intimate level, short-terms for the way in which we may see ourselves, in the sense that we are not isolated entities in an alien environment, but always and inseparably with the world around us as our horizon of meaning. To the extent that I take a derogatory view of myself, I see everything and everyone in the same light as myself, and to the extent that I view my existence as valuable I recognize the other's value as well. This means that it is possible for us to perceive in two different ways, sometimes in an impoverishing, deficiency-causing way, sometimes in an enriching, value awareness. Most of the time, it seems, we perceive in a deficiency-causing way and find it hard to imagine that there are different ways of looking and that there is more to life than what is labelled 'the obvious'.

These two ways of perceiving and the way to effect the transition from an impoverished and impoverishing perception of the world to an enriching awareness of Being are the theme of Saraha's verses:[129]

"I Like a tree overgrown with creepers, the beings
Suffer from thirst in the desert of self-centredness.
Like a prince, homeless and fatherless,
They suffer mental anguish with no chance for happiness.

II The awareness of the Real, that does not come by categorical thinking
Is free from artifacts and is not stored-up Karma.
Thus, I, Saraha, who know it, declare.
Yet the heart of the pedants is filled with poison.

a 1 The peace of Mind-as-such is difficult to understand:
2 Untrammeled by limiting concepts, undefiled, the heart
Can never be investigated concretely in its Being.
3 If it can, it turns into an irritated poisonous snake.
b 1 Things postulated by the intellect are nothing in themselves.
Because they are without foundation, they all do not exist.
2 When one knows the Real free in its reality
Then there is no seeing and no hearing, but also not what is not this.

III All those who believe in concrete things are said to be like cattle,
But those who believe in abstract things are even stupider than these.
Those who use the analogy of a burning lamp and those who use the one of an extinguished lamp
Stay both in Mahāmudrā that knows not of duality.

IV*a* What is born as a thing comes to rest in the no-thing:—
Wise is he who is free from this partiality.
When the fools search their mind with their mind turned inward,
The freedom of that moment is called Dharmakāya.
b Although the simpletons may say: There exists a place
Of Bliss other than this freedom, 'tis like water in a mirage."

The first verse (I) is an apt description of those who suffer, both physically and mentally, when they perceive in a need-determined way, always, always demanding the gratification of their needs that remain unfulfilled because they themselves are unable to give and to share. Karma Phrin-las-pa elaborates on this verse as follows, and it is easy to rediscover in his words the contemporary problem, the feeling of loneliness and alienation:[130]

"A tree overgrown by creepers is an analogy for the beings who through their actions and emotions are fettered in Saṃsāra. Similarly, those whose very being is overgrown, and firmly fettered by the subject-object dichotomy, are tormented by various pains engendered by their belief in a self; suffering from thirst in this desert of misery they experience physical pain and, having no chance for happiness, they experience intense mental anguish. This suffering of body and mind in Saṃsāra is like the unbearable misery a prince with no kingdom and no father has to endure. And this is the nature of Saṃsāra. A forest-tree overgrown by creepers is an analogy for the beings fettered in the world by their actions and emotions; to suffer from thirst in a desert is an analogy for being tormented by the belief in a self. The desert of misery means that as far as the ocean reaches there is no grass, no trees, no sweet water, and in a desert of rocks and sand there are no caves. There, scorched by the sun, one becomes exhausted and wilts like a sprout dried up by the sun.

"The young prince, homeless and fatherless, is an analogy for the suffering in Saṃsāra. Being a 'prince', he had never suffered before, but now in his suffering, like any other common man, he looks run down; and being 'young' he cannot bear the suffering because, unlike an old man, he has not experienced many ups and downs, and does not know how to assess them. 'Homeless' he is not protected by his subjects, and 'fatherless' he is not even sheltered by his next of kin."

The subsequent three verses (II) refer to intrinsic perception, first in a general way and then (*a*1-*b*2) in a more specific way. In explaining these verses Karma Phrin-las-pa speaks of the identity of Being and Awareness and of the resistance which people set up against intrinsic perception. It is the fear of knowledge of oneself. This fear is basically defensive in the sense that it is a means to protect our self-centredness. We are afraid of 'losing ourselves', that is, afraid to see the fictions we have created about ourselves as fictions, and we are also afraid to be. Karma Phrin-las-pa's words are:[131]

> "The objective reference, the absolutely Real, and the owner of the objective reference, the awareness which understands the absolutely Real, are indivisible and this is termed the 'awareness of the Real'. It is the Real and it is Awareness. Saraha declares it to have five characteristics: one may enjoy it as much as one likes and one will never be fed up with it, and since one cannot be fed up with it even after enlightenment one stays with (its) Reality. Since it is not produced by causes and conditions it is without artifacts and it is not Karma stored up by ideas about good and evil. It is to be experienced within ourselves by itself, and it terrifies those doctrinaires who have not practised it. How does it terrify them? To say that the absolutely Real is the indivisibility of objective reference, and owner of the objective reference, is to increase their discomfiture, as if poison enters their heart, because insisting on their difference they cannot bear the dissolution of these two."

Karma Phrin-las-pa then goes on to say that (*a*) intrinsic perception is conceptually incomprehensible and that (*b*) it goes beyond the range of the intellect. Because it is unassailable by concepts it is (1) difficult to understand; (2) concepts cannot exhaust it; and (3) concepts damage it.[132]

"(1) Mind-as-such, the genuine, peace, the presence (of Being), the Real, is difficult to understand by all those who are involved in concepts. Why? Because it is not an object for concepts (which define between them an entity).

"(2) Mind-as-such, untrammeled by all limiting concepts such as eternalism, nihilism, existence, non-existence and so on; the pure Buddhahood potentiality has been intrinsically pure since its (beginningless) beginning, and as it is the very nature of the radiant light it is inaccessible to such concepts as 'deep'. The reason for this statement is given in the next line (3).

"(3) First to conceive of mind as coarse and then as subtle is an artificial procedure and by it the fact of the genuine presence of Being is not understood. It becomes distorted. How? If the fact of the presence of Being is investigated by concepts, not only is it not understood but even tranquillity of mind is not achieved. It becomes like a poisonous snake. As long as a snake is left alone and not irritated it stays happily where it is, but if it is irritated it bites. Similarly, if the presence of Being, mind, is left in its genuine state, it remains undisturbed in the sphere of original awareness, like salt dissolved in water, but if it is investigated conceptually, it is disturbed by them."

Karma Phrin-las-pa here makes it clear that intrinsic or aesthetic perception is 'passive' rather than active, as is ordinary perception, where the beholder chooses what to perceive and relates his selection to his subjective needs, concretizes his percepts and assigns them a reality which they can never have. Such concretizations are the ideas of both object and subject as 'real' entities. About the former (*b*1) Karma Phrin-las-pa says:[133]

> "All that is subsumed under (the categories of) the visible world and its potentiality, under Saṃsāra and Nirvāṇa, is but an interpretative postulate of the intellect; there is not so much as an atom of (independent) reality in these categories. Therefore all these postulates of a visible world

and its possibility are nothing in themselves and since they do not exist at all as they seem to do in the postulate, Saṃsāra and Nirvāṇa, freed from their conceptual inadequacy, are nowhere perceived and are understood as the self-sameness (of Being). Therefore, devoid of their condition, the intellect, all that is postulated by it, becomes free in itself and is not something existing in itself."

About the latter (*b*2) he says:[134]

"Reality is the Real. Free from all concretizations and characterizations, it is real freedom. It is really free and it is Real, and this freely Real is a spontaneous awareness. If one knows it correctly, then there are no concretizations and characterizations as they occur through seeing, hearing and inspecting; and free from seeing and hearing and so on, the subject also is free in itself."

While the previous considerations have shown that Being-as-such is the same as Awareness, the one indicating its existential reality, the other its cognitive one, a new idea is introduced here. This is the idea of freedom as an existential fact, and not as a mere negatively conceived abstraction. We have to remind ourselves here that to be is to be aware, and that in being aware Being exercises its freedom. Freedom is thus synonymous with Being and with Awareness, and is a descriptive term of the functioning of Being as Awareness. From this it follows that 'bondage' is the effect of the functioning of the failure of freedom. This can be illustrated in the following way. In aesthetic experience or intrinsic perception I perceive in a more effortless way, while in ordinary categorical perception I am 'caught' in the fictions of my own making. But this being caught and fettered does not contradict the intrinsic freedom of the noetic functioning. To think of freedom as being something other than the fact of being and of being aware, is to be caught in fictions and in the loss of freedom.

In the following verse (III) Saraha, according to Karma Phrin-las-pa's interpretation, indicates the 'presence' of the Way which, as has been previously shown, is not an inert link between two points, but is the self-manifestation of Being-as-such or, in terms of its cognitiveness, the presence of intrinsic awareness which in its functioning may glide into categorical perception with its postulational affirmations and negations.[135]

"Generally speaking, some people claim that the presence of Being, the absolutely real, is a concrete entity, similar to a burning lamp appearing clearly and concretely before the mind. Thus making an affirmative statement, these people are said to be like cattle, not understanding what presence means. There are others who claim that since the presence of Being cannot be found concretely, it is an abstract entity, similar to a lamp that has been extinguished, not appearing concretely (as burning) before the mind. These Mādhyamika philosophers,[136] making a negative statements, are even stupider than the other people. However, the adherents of a philosophy who, as is evident from the analogies they use, claim the absolutely real to be either a concrete entity or an abstract fact, do not understand the meaning of being free from limitations, because they cling to either appearance or nothingness. Actually, the absolutely real is the spontaneous awareness (in which both, the real and its awareness, are given together), and this is the unsurpassable presence of Being, Mahāmudrā, where concrete things and abstract facts are not existing as two (separate postulates). The meaning is that, since the presence of Being-as-such is free from concretizations and characterizations, to conceive of the Mahāmudrā as a concrete entity is the sign of a stupid person, comparable to an ox. If it is then argued that this presence must be an abstract fact, this idea is even stupider than the previous one because there cannot be an abstract fact in the absence of a negandum. To exemplify, to say that a burning lamp is burning is a silly tautology, but to extinguish a non-burning lamp is even sillier. The word 'both' in Saraha's verse refers to both partisans of the burning lamp and of the extinguished lamp. Thus the Mahāmudrā, existential presence, in which concrete entities and abstract facts do not form a duality, is the genuine, the absolutely real, the Real."

It is on the 'Way' that the human being experiences himself as 'divided against himself', that he is discontented, while at the same time he wants unity. In this respect man is goal-orientated. However, 'goal' must be understood as the possibility or capability of Being to make life meaningful, to 'comprehend' meaning and to be. It is a creative potential but never an end-state. This is precisely what Tantrism is about, and in its own words it claims 'to make the goal the path'. The goal as (*a*) a possibility and (*b*) not as an end-state is the message of Saraha's last (IV) verse:[137]

"*a* Because it is free from what in conceptualization appears as becoming a thing and then as coming to rest in the nothing, the Real, and also from what is conceptualized as the 'no-thing' as contrasted with the 'thing', this knowledge in (its) non-dual awareness, quickly realizes its freedom. If it is argued that there must be a (special) agency to effect this freedom, the answer may be given as follows propositionally: When mind is turned upon itself as it rises unceasingly in the mind of those who are as yet not trained but enjoy the grace of a teacher, the restlessness of the categorical perception of the apparent world gives way to a self-validating aesthetic perception and at that moment gains its freedom. To see the Real, in a manner of not seeing it as something, is said to be seeing the Dharmakayā.

"*b* But does the special experience, of what in the Tantras is said to be unchanging bliss, not contradict Buddhahood? The answer is that although simpletons, who do not know what the real levels (of understanding and the paths to be traversed) mean, may say that there is a level of great bliss, which is different from the freedom in self-validating aesthetic perception, it does not exist as such and is but like the water in a mirage. Therefore in the Tantras self-validating awareness is termed absolute bliss."

Karma Phrin-las-pa's detailed interpretation of Saraha's verses reveals the importance aesthetic perception has in Tantrism, because it is through this perception that more of what there is can be seen. However, aesthetic perception is not an end in itself but a means of becoming aware of one's Being. If it were an end in itself it would result in the sentimentality of the kind of aestheticism that, instead of enriching a man's life, actually impoverishes it due to the demand it makes on the objects. Aesthetic perception as a means towards gaining an existential awareness recognizes the world appearing to our senses as being there and, in bringing about an enhanced vision, it reveals the limitations of categorical perception and its deadening effects. But if it is taken as an end in itself, it has the same effect as categorical perception. Saraha and Karma Phrin-las-pa leave no doubt about this:

> "The awareness that is not differentiated and alone
> Is encompassed by the mind left in itself.
> Knowing that what appears as oneself and the other is one actuality,
> Hold to this alone by not moving away from it;
> But since this same act may be the mind's torment, renounce it
> And deal with anything in bliss supreme without attachment."

The unitary awareness which is one's own mind if it is 'let alone' can well be understood as a peak experience, but when it is taken to be an end in itself it is no longer 'left alone', and in the difference that is set up between subject and object all the torment that usually accompanies the rift in Being asserts itself. In this sense the peak experience may well be the opposite of what it promises. Karma Phrin-las-pa has this to say by way of explanation:[138]

> "The awareness in the self-validating aesthetic experience in which there is no differentiation into self and other, subject and object, Saṃsāra and Nirvāṇa, is the sole bliss supreme. This is to be understood as permeating itself with bliss supreme, through the mind that has settled in its genuine and original state. When one first has recognized that the actuality of all that appears in a dual way, due to the postulates of a self and another, has but one flavour, one should hold unswervingly in full concentration to this one-flavoured actuality. But this same concentration turns

> out to be a torment to lower minds, and therefore, according to the words 'give it up when there is attachment',[139] one should get rid of this attachment and only then can one deal with anything without attachment in this bliss supreme that is individually experienced as self-validating."

There is no doubt that aesthetic perception as an end in itself fails miserably in what it sets out to do, to enrich perception and, by implication, to make a person learn more about his Being which he shares with everybody else and everything else. Since all and everything both represents and constitutes Being, it becomes a 'teacher' in the sense that it makes one realize Being through accepting what there is:

> "When one looks at all and everything when pointed out
> There is nothing that does not become a teacher.
> The sky, pointed out by a finger, does not see the sky,
> 'Tis the same with the teacher pointed out by the teacher."

says Saraha, and Karma Phrin-las-pa comments:[140]

> " 'All and everything' is an intensifying phrase and will say that nothing has been left out. Therefore, when one looks at the whole of the phenomenal world as constituting an existential presence, when the teacher points it out, at the moment of the self-validating awareness there is nothing that does not become the teacher of this existential presence. In the *People Dohā*[141] it is said:
>
> Seeing, hearing, touching, thinking,
> Eating, smelling, running, walking, sitting,
> Idly talking, talking back—
> Know all this to be the mind and do not run from this oneness. To see Being is not to see it as something. In the same way as the sky pointed out to a child with the finger, does not see the sky in the manner of subject and object, so also the spontaneous awareness, the teacher, pointed out by the teacher, is seen in a non-dual manner."

But if anything and everything in the phenomenal world to which I belong by my being embodied in it, and which at any level constitutes my horizon of meaning, can teach me about my existential values, how much more is this possible through interpersonal relationships and their emotional conditions that affect the ways of knowing? A person who is attached to, or hates, another, remains not only ignorant of the other, who for him is not a genuine person, but a segment that is selectively, classificatorily distorted by his own feelings, but he remains equally ignorant of himself. Treating others as mere objects he turns himself into a mere object for others, dispensable, and the quicker done away with the better. Inter-personal relationships require existential knowledge rather than categorical, 'objective', knowledge. It is here that the change from the boredom with the 'dead' object to the appreciation of an alive person, the transmutation of dry facts into values, becomes most marked. The change, not only in attitude, but also in the actual action, is again the theme of Saraha's words: [142]

> "A yogi keeping his observances while thinking of a village
> Enters a king's palace and in dallying with the princess,
> Like a man who has tasted bitter food assumes all other food to be bitter,
> Is aware of everything as (exemplifying) the presence of Being."

One of the striking features in the imagery employed is the disparity in status, the inequality of the yogi and the king and his daughter, the humble village and the gorgeous palace. This thesis implies a kind of knowledge which recognizes this inequality as long as the objective scrutiny lasts. But there also is implied another kind of knowledge which recognizes the existential quality which does not negate the things observed, but lets their disparity and difference fade into the background and lets the two perceptual forces fuse creatively for the enhancement of the awareness. The importance of change and transmutation, hierarchically organized, is elaborated by Karma Phrin-las-pa: [143]

> "The literal interpretation is that a yogi, who has understood the meaning of existential presence and acts in accordance with his vows, may think of villages and other temporary places of residence and wandering from one place to another happen to enter the palace of a king. Even when he dallies with the princess he is not affected.

Just as a man who has previously tasted some bitter food will see any other food as tasting bitter, so (the yogi) seeing the external objects, colour-form and so on, will be intrinsically aware of them in their existential value. The exoteric interpretation is: A yogi who has subdued evil and has punctiliously set out on the path to liberation, thinks of the hamlets of ordinary persons as impermanent abodes. Entering unsurpassable enlightenment, the palace of the Buddha, King of Dharma, even when he, wise in appropriate action, amuses himself with the princess, the *prajñāpāramitā*, like a man who previously has tasted some bitter food and sees all food as tasting bitter, will experience all the objects of senses such as colours, sounds, and so on, as existential values.

"The esoteric interpretation is: A yogi who has overcome specific modes of behaviour and engages in a non-specific one, thinks of the inner and outer world as the abode of 'heroes' and 'ḍākas' and, entering the great mystic circle, the palace of Vajradhara, king of gods, he, wise in the ways of mysticism, amuses himself with the princess Nairātmyā, and knows everything as existentially real.

"This may suffice as an example of the many explanations possible."

Human relations differ in degrees of intimacy; this applies in particular to sexual relations which can be extremely casual or an inseparable part of very deep human relationship. The physical aspect is never *merely* physical, but always expressive of meaning, although this is not often realized.

Inasmuch as sexuality expresses Being, as has been shown above, in its expression it at once becomes the battleground of two conflicting attitudes which may be termed as a Being-orientated attitude and an ego-centred attitude. The Being-attitude is more likely to recognize sexuality and, in this recognition, runs the risk of reducing Being to some sort of being, and of absolutizing it. The ego-centred attitude is more likely to reject sexuality because it poses a threat to the ego which is felt to be lost or 'transcended' in the sexual experience, and, in its rejection, the ego-centred attitude becomes destructive of itself and of others. Every society consists of individuals who adopt certain attitudes, and the life of any society seems to depend on the interaction of the extreme attitudes of either glorifying or denouncing sex. However, in the ultimate analysis there is little difference between glorification and denunciation, in either case something or other has been singled out and abstracted from Being and turned into an obsession. In the one case, the person is obsessed to get more and more out of it, in the other to make less and less of it. The common denominator for both activities is the orgy, an excessive indulging in any particular action. In the narrower sense of sexual activity orgies developed in the wake of fertility cults which were a kind of sympathetic magic to 'help life on', and in this respect became a correlate to asceticism as a means to make an end of life.

Orgies have been part of life in India since earliest times and are not a particular feature of Tantrism. But since Tantrism stayed alive long after the great philosophical systems had exhausted themselves in sterile abstractions, on the basis of ignorance about the historical scene, the impression has been created that orgies and Tantrism in some way or other belonged together. Moreover, since sex is the source of life and an orgy more an outgrowth, and since a life-affirming attitude in its acceptance of life in all its vagaries is likely to assume that life will eventually adjust itself, the Indians did not feel called upon to give this outgrowth undue attention, unlike the established church in the West with its political ties and aims, which true to its life-denying spirit, celebrated orgies of persecution and extermination of those who showed any regard for life in any form, as is exemplified by the Albigensian Crusade, the Inquisition and other unsavoury activities. There is a tremendous difference, however, between orgies as outgrowth of sexuality and sexual relationship as a means of self-growth. The main point of an orgy is not to know who one's partner is, and when the other has no identity, not only does one's own identity not get any buttressing from the other but one also has none oneself. Everyone is, as it were, drowned in a common pool of anonymity. Sex as a means towards self-growth also tears down the barriers of selfhood, but there is as much dissolving as tempering. The reaction which is the interaction between man and woman and, in a wider horizon, Saṃsāra and Nirvāṇa, becomes unitary, not diverse; compound rather than mixed. The 'self', for want of a better term in English, that emerges is thus a compound of two factors, man and woman, neither of which separately has the characteristic properties of a 'self', just as salt is a compound of two substances, neither of which by itself has the characteristic properties of salt. However, it would be unwise to press the analogy to chemical compounds too far. So far as we know, no permanent change is produced in the properties of either chemical element when they are united to form a compound. In the human sphere both man and woman seem to be permanently affected by their union, so that, if they become separated again and continue to live apart, their 'properties' are characteristically different from what they were when the two became connected with each other. This consideration may help to understand what sex as a unifying symbol in Tantrism is about. Saraha says:[144]

> "In a place emblazoned by the *gaṇacakra*
> The yogis (and yoginīs) during the act of copulation
> Witness bliss supreme and through symbols and commitment
> Are tempered into Mahāmudrā, the self-sameness of Saṃsāra and Nirvāṇa."

Karma Phrin-las-pa gives four interpretations, each one following out of the other:[145]

> "The literal explanation is as follows: In a selected spot which is 'emblazoned by the *gaṇacakra*', the assemblage of yogis and yoginīs who have received their empowerments and are keeping their commitments, these yogis and yoginīs seeing the birth of bliss supreme in their act of copulation, when each one unites with his or her partner, through the exchange of symbols and enacting their commitments, are tempered into Mahāmudrā, the vision of Saṃsāra and Nirvāṇa as alike. The exoteric explanation is as follows: The accumulation (*gaṇa*) of appropriate action and appreciative awareness as forming a unity is similar to

cakra, because it overcomes what is adverse. In a secluded and pleasant place 'emblazoned by this *gaṇacakra*' when Being is seen, symbolized by the act of copulation, the yogis and yoginīs, witnessing the birth of bliss supreme in their self-validating intrinsic awareness, see through their expertise in symbols and action and their enactment of the commitments, Saṃsāra and Nirvāṇa as alike in their unreality. Since this vision is the path to the union with Mahāmudrā they will temper all that is into a unity.

"The esoteric explanation is as follows: Coition takes place in the 'conch', the lower end of the central structural pathway, a place enriched by four or six focal points of experience surrounded by countless delicate channels.[146] The yogis and yoginīs, witnessing the ever-growing intensity of bliss supreme during their experience of spontaneous pleasure, rely on the symbols of the four joys and the Samayamudrā combining the 'white' and 'red' energies, and understand Saṃsāra and Nirvāṇa as alike in bliss and openness. Since this is the way to Mahāmudrā they temper everything into self-sameness of bliss and openness.

"The explanation from an ultimate point of view is as follows: Since the assemblage (*gaṇa*) of symbols and appropriate actions destroys the fetters of the conceptual fictions it is a *cakra*. 'Emblazoned by it' means that appropriate action is not divorced from absolute compassionateness. Coition is the union with the Karmamudrā; the awareness in self-validating intrinsic perception, symbolized by the vision of the birth of bliss supreme. 'Symbol' means openness of Being and 'enacting the commitment' means to have absolute compassionateness. Therefore, the yogi who is aware of the unity of appropriate action and appreciative awareness understands the self-sameness of intrinsic awareness and openness; intrinsic awareness being a symbol for Saṃsāra and openness for Nirvāṇa. Since this understanding is Mahāmudrā they temper everything into the self-sameness of intrinsic awareness and openness."

It will have been noted that in all these passages emphasis is on knowledge, appreciative rather than cumulative, and on unity. Stress is laid upon knowledge through personal encounter (Karmamudrā, Jñānamudrā) and upon the need for involvement in order to know (*snyoms-par 'jug-pa*), though not as an end in itself. This makes knowledge existential and it must be realized in personal time-consuming experience. The unity of this existential knowledge cannot be stated adequately at all, because the individuality of the experience is in conflict with the generality of conceptual language. Traditionally it has been assumed that it is possible to contemplate body, mind, life, value, man and woman conceptually as objects and all that was necessary for a final presentation of a world picture was to think them together. It is now realized that there is a need to experience and to understand as far as we can not only these 'entities' through a knowledge gained in direct relationship, by being involved with them, but also these in relation to each other.

> "Without knowing the concrete existential presence of the body as the bearer (of psychical life) one does not understand the concrete existential presence of the mind as (the life existing in the body)."[147]

says Padma dkar-po, and after quoting a few passages from the Buddhist scriptures in support of his statement he continues:[148]

> "When by knowing the body as the bearer (of psychical life) the place of the mind (resting on it) is known, it is through an involvement that a realization necessarily springs up. To give an example, although milk pervades the body of a cow, you can get it from the udder, not from the horns."

Thus, in order to understand body and mind, man and woman, or Saṃsāra and Nirvāṇa, as different parts of some complex unified knowledge, it is necessary to know them existentially one by one, to know them existentially in their relationship, and to know their unity. This does not happen in a haphazard way, but through feeling, acting, thinking, which is the 'Way' as a process of unification. The result, the unity of knowledge, is then not a constructed intellectual schema but a personal acquisition,

XI. Sahaja (lhan-cig-skyes-pa): Symbol of spontaneity and ecstatic bliss (*Author's collection*)

XII. White Tārā [white: colour of great compassion] (*Author's collection*)

a living state of mind which can be recognized and known, but which defies all conceptual statements. Even to speak of it as an acquisition is already saying too much.

When we speak of the way as a process of unification, and if we want to understand what this existentiality means, we have to remind ourselves of the fact that unification presupposes the existence of diversity, of plurality, and that it is the *existence* of plurality that does not contradict unity. Plurality, correctly understood, never means (and never can mean) isolatedness. Whatever *is*, is diverse, but not isolated in the sense of being unrelated to whatever else there is. Each individual has its specific position or quality in relation to all other individuals in a continuous actuality of this relationship. Unity is constituted in the plurality of subjects as the world, which is not a duality of subject and object, but is this plurality of subjects (individuals). Unity also is not totality in the sense that the world is made up of isolated individuals or that it is divided up into isolated (unrelated) individuals. Unity is neither outside nor above nor beyond plurality; it is not a 'one' from which the 'many' can be speculatively derived.

Experienced unity is termed Mahāmudrā which is then said to comprise the ground, the path, and the goal. With the Mahāmudrā idea we come to the very core of Tantrism, and without grasping this central problem all talk about Tantrism remains meaningless. We have to start with what is certain, that is, Being(-as-such) is and Being is Awareness. Awareness is both knowledge and evaluation. In knowing (something) I not only notice something but also express an opinion about it, and in so evaluating it, my knowledge or rather my opinion determines my life. However, opinion is not knowledge in the strict sense of the word; it deals with what seemingly is and it always is ego-centred. Opinion is subjective in a derogatory sense; its 'knowledge' is a make-belief knowledge. Contrariwise, insight does not deal with what seemingly is (for me), but with what really is, with Being-as-such; it is not added to Being but already contained in it in the sense that Being is being-aware, regardless of what the content of this awareness may be. Awareness thus is the function*ing* of

Being. In being aware I am always aware of something, which means that to be is to have object. But since there can be no other being than Being-as-such without invalidating what is certain, namely, that Being is, and since in being-aware I am aware of an object as being, it follows that if the object is to be, it must be so as having object, too; but in view of the fact that there can be only Being-as-such, the object must have the primary subject as object. Moreover, while the subject-object relationship is unequivocal, and while the subject in its functioning (being aware) expresses various opinions about the object, multiplicity is found in the object. If on the basis of these considerations we let A stand for Being-as-such as subject, and B for the object it has, and Bc, Bd and so on for the multiplicity of the object in the functioning of the subject, and if we let A 1 stand for the object which because of its being must be subject having B, and Bc_1 Bd_1 and so on as its object which is existentially the primary subject A, we get the following formula of Being and/or Awareness:

$$\begin{array}{rcl} & A \longrightarrow & B\ (Bc,\ Bd,\ \ldots) \\ & & \| \\ (\ldots\ldots\ Bd_1\ Bc_1)\quad B & \longleftarrow & A\,1 \end{array}$$

Without ever leaving the object behind (which is existentially impossible) the subject can 'express an opinion' or 'gain insight', and it can do so in utter freedom. Freedom is the enactment of being aware, the free functioning of Being-as-such as an available possibility. Realization of the possibilities of Being-as-such is the 'path' which is not something apart from Being, but Being in transformation.

Transformation is activity. It happens through Being, the subject is not changed but always changes in the act of expressing an opinion or gaining insight. In other words, to be is always to become. Being is not something behind Becoming, it *is* becom*ing*. In becoming, the subject enters a new state, 'reaches a goal', but this new state is always *its* state. This does not contradict the statement that there is 'no transmigration and change' (*'pho-'gyur med-pa*). Being does not step out of itself into something which it is not, nor does it change into something which it is not.

Therefore Mahāmudrā has no beginning and no end; 'beginning' and 'end' belong to speculation, not to Being.

"There is neither beginning, middle, nor end,
'Tis neither a Saṃsāraless Nirvāṇa.
In this supreme bliss unsurpassed
There is no self or other,"

says Saraha.

We have seen that the 'goal' is not to be understood as an end-state;[149] consequently Mahāmudrā also is not an end-state, once there and for ever, but as its etymology indicates, it 'seals' and the outcome is Samayamudrā:

"In front and in the rear and in the ten directions
Whatever one sees is It,
By this day, a master, I have destroyed error:
Now I need not ask anyone."

gNyis-med Avadhūtipa explains this verse in terms of symbols of Buddhahood which is Being as Awareness, never an absorption in a lifeless fiction. Buddhahood is in the world in the sense that the world represents Buddhahood and in its existence constitutes it. Thus gNyis-med Avadhūtipa says:[150]

"Since there is appearance of multiplicity through the (activity of our) present 'memory', there is Vairocana in front; since on the other side 'non-memory' pervades appearance, there is Amitābha in the rear; since out of their indivisibility, like (from) the Wish-Fulfilling Gem, there arises a multiplicity (of values), there is Ratnasambhava; since this multiplicity of values assists the sentient beings, there is Amoghasiddhi; since (all this) has not moved from its being, there is Akṣobhya. The understanding that Saṃsāra and Nirvāṇa as well as the fact that they have no 'cause' derive from a single 'cause' is kindliness. To make understood what has not yet been understood is appropriate action or compassion. To have understood and not to be separated (from Being) is joy; the fact that this transcends the subjective mind is equanimity. Since all this is not relativistically subjective, this is Vajrasattva. This is the ten (directions). Wherever one looks one does not move away from Being. Hence Saraha's words: In front and in the rear and in the ten directions."

The symbolism used here is, one might say, on a cosmic scale. Vairocana, literally translated, means the 'Illuminator', and its Tibetan translation, literally rendered, means 'making appear in observable qualities'; and the association with 'memory' which is a symbol term for our ordinary mental activities, like apprehending, remembering, inspecting, judging, noticing, indicates the vividness of the experience of observing the azure of waters, the luxuriance of the fields and forests, the radiance of the mountains with their snow-caps, the gracefulness of the movement and the loveliness of body of the living beings. But although all this is observable, there is in it a hidden charm, intangibly secret and yet ever-present, all pervasive. If we want to say something about it we must speak in negative terms, because all positive terms exclude and reduce. Thus, the ever-present openness of Being is 'non-memory' and as an inner glow Amitābha, an infinite light. Wherever we see something there is this indivisibility of observable qualities and their open dimension which is felt as a value, a treasure both to be cherished and to be used to enrich ourselves and the world. This, then, is Ratnasambhava, a mine of jewels. This richness of sensibility makes for fullness of life, meaningfulness of action in the light of Being, and therefore is Amoghasiddhi, 'unfailingly successful'. Such an existential awareness is an unshakable insight, fittingly symbolized by Akṣobhya, 'the immovable and undisturbable'. But when we perceive, fascinated by the charm and beauty of what there is, when our perception of the intrinsic qualities of what there is grows ever more profound, we can be all-loving and be all-kindliness. The reaction to the world is not one of blame or condemnation but of assisting. This is compassion. Its action is based on the recognition of the other's Being and value, and being based on knowledge it is not a cheap sentimentalism with which it is confused by ignorance. Another value of the understanding of Being is joyfulness. Joy is the natural expression of the feeling of unity, and while kindliness and compassion are more outwardly directed, joy and equanimity are inwardly directed. Equanimity is the acceptance of what there is as it is in its Being. It is said to 'transcend subjective mind' because our subjectivism just cannot accept things as they are, they always must be for some purpose or other. Subjectivism prevents us from 'enjoying' and from 'caring'. Joy is not the same as 'having a good time' and equanimity is not indifference which, summed up in the motto 'I couldn't care less', illustrates the contempt for Being which, as the above analysis shows, is never a static and soporific state. Conceptual language can never do justice to the living experience: at its best it can point. It can point to the unity of Being by saying that Being is one, but has many facets—Vajrasattva.

gNyis-med-Advadhūtipa gives still another interpretation which, as it were, brings the matter 'closer home'. He relates Vairocana and the other symbols to the traditional five constituents that make up a living individual and to five 'spiritual' phenomena. Here, Vairocana and so on are symbols of unity. The following diagram will assist in assessing the problems involved:

corporeality	Vairocana	ethics
feeling	Ratnasambhava	concentration
concept-formation	Amitābha	appreciation
motivated action	Amoghasiddhi	freedom
perceptual judgments	Akṣobhya	vision in freedom and pristine awareness

The five items in the column to the left are also the five kinds of original awareness (*ye-shes*) that constitute the aspects of Buddhahood-awareness. The first item, corporeality (*rūpa*), refers to our body as lived and as 'perceived'. As can easily be ascertained, we perceive our body not so much as a three-dimensional physical object, but as a Gestalt, a pattern of form and colour. It is by means of this pattern that there are other sensuously perceivable and practico-instrumental patterns in the world. In this sense our body is an 'illuminator' (Vairocana) and through it as an orientational point the spatio-temporal surrounding world is organized around it, and in this sense also the body is a means of perception and awareness (*ye-shes*). Another point to be remembered is that 'body' in Tantric thought is 'embodiment'. As such it is active and tendential. When we look at man in this way, we focus not so much on *what* he is but on *how* he acts. Inasmuch as the body is awareness in the above sense and inasmuch as sound insight (knowledge, not opinion) and appropriate action (ethics) reinforce each other, ethics is an 'illuminator' as well. The more I misunderstand myself as a mere thing, the more degraded action becomes, for being valueless myself everything else is equally valueless, and if I am but dust, how else can I convince myself of it but by reducing everything (and above all, everybody else) to dust? But to the extent that I take a healthier and more positive view of myself and of what there is in relation to myself, my actions become ennobled. Thus there is a correlative and unity between my bodily existence and my ethical actions.

Feeling, too, is a kind of awareness and has its own peculiar mode of disclosure of how it is going with me. Not only has every action its feeling tone, every cognition has its mood. Usually we deny feelings any cognitive significance and tend to dismiss them as purely subjective, ego-centred. It is true, most of our perception and experience is filtered through our system of categories, schematizations, classifications and generalizations, and in comparing, approving, condemning, relating, we usually have 'strong feelings' about our ideas. In other words, feeling is highly differentiated with reference to the external reference in a perceptual or cognitive situation. Such feelings, of course, are unstable and transitory. On the other hand, in aesthetic experience where the object is perceived as if it were all there is in the world, and where it loses its thing-character, feeling also is free from the narrowness of specific practical connection; it becomes less and less differentiated and more and more approximates pure feeling or 'bliss supreme'. To perceive something intrinsically, as if it were all that is, is concentration, an attention to something in its being and value. This is felt as an enrichment (Ratnasambhava), and it also explains the rich contribution of Buddhist Tantrism to the fine arts. Its paintings and sculptures possess a totality of expressed feeling and have an intrinsic perceptual appeal.

Ordinary perception is largely determined by or mixed with concepts. These are basically principles of interpretations which we apply to what we perceive by our senses. Concepts are 'put into' the experience, not derived from it. For instance, the concept 'physical object' is defined by a set of postulates or propositions, and a 'physical object' just is something that answers to this set. Whatever doubts we may harbour about concepts when we reflect on them, we act and go on acting as if we believed in them unquestionably. Concepts, such as 'physical object', throw light (Amitābha) on our 'physical world'. However, we also perceive qualities such as a timbre, a texture, a brilliant flash of colours around us for their intrinsic character. Such tiny instances of aesthetic experience not only add variety to our routine existence, they also throw light (Amitābha) on our world. Appreciation is simply perception given major scope, depth, and value. A person who can appreciate does not see what others are unable to see, but he sees more of what all of us ordinarily see.

Inasmuch as concepts are principles of interpretation, they exert their influence on our actions. In this respect all our actions are motivated and reinforced by the 'strong feelings' we have about our ideas. If I 'think' that everything and everyone is my 'enemy' I will infallibly (Amoghasiddhi) set out to destroy what endangers my ego, but since this may be too egocentric and hence not socially acceptable, I 'think' of generalities, as for instance, genocide for the sake of national security, and I can be quite sanctimonious about it because there is no better way to show my contempt for the flesh, and no better licence to enforce this creed than to quote, possibly out of context, the words 'I came not to bring peace but the sword'. On the other hand, if I think of the other in his Being and value, I am more likely to appreciate, to be kind and compassionate to him or her, because I *know* how it feels to be. Whatever action, positive or negative, I perform is the exercise of (existential) freedom (Amoghasiddhi).

Our conscious world is made up of judgments of perception which assume the character of unassailability and unshakableness (Akṣobhya); and while we interpret by means of our concepts, we also have a vision of reality in its freedom from the narrowness of practical concerns, and in pristine awareness. This is an existential unshakableness (Akṣobhya), free from the limitations that judgments impose on us, and so intrinsically aware.

These symbols of unity are hierarchically organized and held together by another symbol of unity. This may seem to be purely speculative, but actually it is a linguistic accident. We cannot express the complexity of Being without splitting it up into a number of partial symbols. Advayavajra explains:[151]

> "The five psycho-physical constituents are five Tathāgatas. Have the first four been 'sealed' by Akṣobhya in order to make it clear that there is only original awareness? By this sealing is shown that in the absence of external objects there can be no subject and that therefore perception as pure sensation in an absolute sense, devoid of any external and internal reference, exists. This is like the clear sky at noon in autumn and is accepted as the basic awareness by the (Yogācāra-philosophers) who claim absence of observable qualities. As has been stated:
>
> Devoid of any fictional content, without delusive appearance or form,
> It is pure sensation in an ultimate sense, later it becomes distracted by observable qualities.
>
> It also has been stated that the two Rūpakāyas are subsequent, hence:
>
> Inaccessible to propositions, without observable qualities is the Dharmakāya of the Great Sage,
> The two Rūpakāyas derive from it like an apparition.
>
> If this is established by the Akṣobhya-seal, why is Akṣobhya sealed by Vajrasattva? If it only means once again to establish the fact that there are no fictional contents, this is redundant because it has already been done so by the previous seal. However, in the same way that by the Akṣobhya-seal it has been established that awareness is basic and everything else subsequent, so by the Vajrasattva-seal it is established that Being (Vajra) is basic and perception subsequent. In the *Vajraśekhara* it has been said:
>
> It is firm, round, cannot be changed, be pierced, be split,
> Cannot be burnt, is indestructible and (as) openness it is called Vajra."

The statement that awareness is basic and everything else subsequent, or that Being is basic and awareness subsequent, does not contradict the initial fact that Being is awareness and vice versa. The difference, if any, lies in the approach to the ontological problem involved. The metaphysician is more likely to explain Being, while the speculative philosopher is likely to concentrate on the working of Mind.

This difference of approach is again noticeable in the terms Samāyāmudrā and Phalamudrā. The latter, used by Nāropa, focuses on unity as a crowning achievement, while the term Samāyāmudrā implies the commitment to Being through the symbols of unity. Nāropa reflects more the speculative side of Tantric thought, while gNyis-med Avadhūtipa and others, using the term Samāyāmudrā, emphasize the existential nature of unity and the obligations that derive from it. Still the existential importance is not missing in Nāropa's words:[152]

> "Phalamudrā is the bliss of Mahāmudrā. Its characteristic is an original awareness in (a state of) ultimate and immutable bliss. All the time it carries with it pleasure, because the previous state (the Mahāmudrā experience) has been made stable. Hence it is called mudrā (seal, encounter, indelible impression). Its greatness consists in greatness of riddance and greatness of possession. Greatness of riddance is the realization of the lucency of intrinsic Being (*svābhāvikakāya*) which is characterized by the riddance of all tendencies and all veils. Greatness of possession is the realization of unitive Being (*yuganaddha*), the pure nature of all Buddhas."

Unitive Being is Dharmakāya, as Nāropa points out:[153]

> "That which is by nature the non-duality of the Two Truths is called Unitive Being. Therefore unitive Being is Dharmakāya."

And Advayavajra states:[154]

> "It has never come into existence because it is not something.
> And it never ceases because it is present under specific conditions.

Therefore existence and non-existence are not (separate) existents,
They are a unity.
The oneness of openness (of Being) and compassion
Is unanalyzable in terms of one's fictions.
There is unity by nature
Of Openness and Manifestedness."

He takes up this idea in his discussion of the symbol Vajrasattva:[155]

"By Vajra openness is meant, by Sattva original awareness:
Their identity is Vajrasattva.
The difference between openness (of Being) and Compassion is like that between the lamp and its light;
The openness of openness (of Being) and Compassion is like that of the lamp and its light.
Openness is not different from what there is, and what there is is never without openness.
The fact that the one is not without the other is like the going together of the artificial and the genuine.
In the light of absoluteness there is no end of relativity,
Apart from relativity there is no absoluteness."

With these words Advayavajra clearly outlines the metaphysical position of Buddhist Tantrism. Whatever we encounter is relative to something else, mountains are relative to valleys, days to nights. This fact we call 'relativity'. But relativity is itself not relative to something, and this we call 'absoluteness'. The absoluteness of Being is the relativity of what there is. But what we discuss in cold intellectual terms, Advayavajra can present in a deeply moving image:[156]

"The world of appearance is a loving husband,
but only relatively.
If he were not, his loving wife, the openness
(of Being) would be dead.
If the lovely, loving openness, in beauty unsurpassed,
Were at any time alone, her loving husband would be fettered.
They once hesitatingly approached the Guru

Who through their mutual amorousness made them
experience spontaneous love."

While the rapture of the attainment of unity, the release from both inner and outer conflicts, may make us oblivious to the fact that we are beings embodied in a world of our interpretations, the Samāyāmudrā commits us to our Being which is never some mysterious entity above or beyond the ordinary world in which we live, but is this same world changed to the extent that we ourselves have changed, by having moved from the periphery to the centre. To live in the world, by body, speech and mind, but committed to Being, is the theme of Saraha's verses according to gNyis-med Avadhūtipa's commentary. Saraha says:

"1 Where the senses pass away
And where the essence fails,
Friends, that is (your) spontaneous bodily existence.
Ask the Guru clearly.
2 Where the subjective disposition is suspended and where motility fades out,
There all potentialities are present.
The ignorant imagine it as a border-line,
But for those who know it by having exhausted the ocean of ignorance—
3 This is bliss supreme, unmatched.
Saraha has shown it and has gone."

The first verse refers to one's spontaneous bodily existence which gNyis-med Avadhūtipa elucidates in various ways. The first thing to note is that 'body' is a dynamic pattern, 'creative' as embodiment, and not primarily the various organs. Serving as an analogy by shifting our attention from categorical postulates to an intrinsic perception, it facilitates our understanding of two aspects involved in intrinsic perception. gNyis-med Avadhūtipa's words are:[157]

> "One's indirect spontaneous bodily existence is the two creative polarities, in which the sensory organs do not exist. One's concrete spontaneous bodily existence can be viewed in two ways, indirectly and concretely. The indirect one is tendential and non-tendential. The tendential one

means that when we perceive it as a percept, a Gestalt, then it has neither flesh nor blood nor sense organs. The non-tendential one means that it has no sense organs because it is not even seen as a Gestalt. This real body, which is present throughout time in its self-sameness as it is not subject to the three aspects of time, is pointed out by the true Guru in tradition. Hence Saraha says: When the senses pass away. Since here no essence associated with a self and its ascriptions is found, Saraha continues: And when the essence fails.

"Those who do not understand that the intentionality of Buddhahood throughout time is not something that can be subjectivated, befriend evil, because subjectivism cannot find deliverance from Saṃsāra. Those who understand that spontaneity as the ultimately real is not subjectivism, are helpful friends, hence Saraha's words: Friend, that is your spontaneous bodily existence.

"Simultaneously with the instruction by the vision of the face of the true Guru in tradition, and without asking for indirect spontaneity, since spontaneity depends on the true Guru, Saraha concludes: Ask the Guru clearly."

The distinction between 'the true Guru in tradition' and 'the concrete Guru' is of singular importance. The true Guru is Being-as-such which speaks to us through symbols as concrete contents of our mind. These concrete symbols are the symbols of unity which, as Vairocana and others, impress on us the need to preserve our integrity at all times and under all circumstances. Figuratively we, too, say: 'to come face to face with . . .' and in such moments we are called upon to act in the light of Being, rather than in the darkness of our intervening concepts. In such moments also we do not even perceive our bodily existence in terms of a Gestalt, and least of all in terms of a three-dimensional physical object answering a set of postulates.

Speech is geared to our concepts and is unable to express the ineffable which, far from being of a speculative nature for which there is no specific criterion of verification, can be immediately experienced. It will help when we distinguish between talk and communication. Talk—"a barren superfluity of words"—is detracting from the problem of being, while, in communication, Being may communicate itself to us and through us to others. gNyis-med Avadhūtipa says:[158]

> "Speech consists of vowels and consonants and depends on the subjective disposition and motor-activity. It searches with words for the real, but the real is inexpressible. To illustrate this by means of indirect spontaneity, when in between the polarizing streams of creativity the motility of the subjective disposition is not operative, appearance (depending on this activity) disappears, but openness does not rise. Similarly, in real communication the motility of subjective disposition, mind, perception, judgments of perception—is not active. Hence Saraha says: When the subjective disposition is arrested and when motility fades out.
>
> "Since this point becomes the foundation for existentiality, the positive qualities of Buddhahood, Saraha continues: There all potentialities are present.
>
> "As what can this be known? That which is the ineffable in between the polarities of individual creativity, sun and moon, is known as the border-line between 'memory' and 'non-memory', the real creativity. Saraha says (of this concretization): The ignorant imagine it as a border-line. But by knowing what is not perception and perceived content, as profound and ineffable, the ocean of ignorance has been exhausted."

Our body as an 'expression' of psychic life, tending to communicate itself through verbal patterns which help to turn the 'body' into concepts, points to the mind which is in the images of the mind and the tendencies of experience. In this way it is already a 'formulated', 'conditioned' mind rather than the awareness of Being and the Being of awareness. So gNyis-med Avadhūtipa declares:[159]

> "Our present mind is altered by conditions and tendencies of experience and therefore is known only indirectly. The real mind remains unaltered and is without (altering)

concepts. Its conceptlessness has never been sullied by the mire of accidental 'memory' and 'non-memory', but as Saraha explains: This is bliss supreme, unmatched.

"Where the yogis, who understand this, go to, is pointed out in the instruction which says: 'Where (the concept)-body evaporates there is Nirmāṇakāya, where talk evaporates there is Sambhogakāya, and where subjectivism evaporates there is Dharmakāya.' Hence Saraha's words: Saraha has shown it and has gone."

It is a recurrent theme that conceptualization leads us away from the immediacy and uniqueness of Being, because having a concept of something we attribute to Being the characteristics of which we have the concept. This is to limit Being, for to say that Being possesses characteristic A is to say that it lacks the characteristic not-A, but then to say that it is limitless is to do so not a whit less. Even to say that it is existing is still to say something about it, even if existence is not an attribute, because we use a concept to refer to it, and concepts tend to obliterate uniqueness. However, every direct and immediate experience is unique and spontaneous, and this is most obvious in a love experience, an aesthetic experience, and in the burst of insight. While conceptualization occurs in the wake of selfish cognition, in which the world is organized into what gratifies or frustrates our selfish needs and where everything is a means to other means which, in turn, are means to other means *ad infinitum*, spontaneity is part of a total situation and the individual's total response to a particular situation at a particular moment. This is its originality and freshness; only egocentricity is repetitive, stale, and neurotic. While it may not be possible to describe accurately how it feels to have a peak-experience or 'to be', the rich imagery used by those who have had the experience may help to lead people to, and finally to evoke within them, those experiences which have been considered to be the most worth while of all experiences by those who have had them. Saraha exclaims:

"Indeed, this is self-validating awareness.
Do not become alienated from it!
Things and no-things fetter Buddhahood;

Without making a difference between world and self-sameness,
Let the genuine subject stay alone, o yogi!
Know this to be like water poured into water."

gNyis-med Avadhūtipa explains this verse as follows:[160]

"As to the real, there is no alienation. If this is not understood there is alienation due to the alienating activity of 'memory'. When it is understood, 'memory' becomes purified and there is no doubt as to what does not turn into an object of subjective mind. Hence Saraha says: Do not become alienated from it!

"The intentionality of Buddhahood throughout time is fettered by the concept 'thing', so also it is by the concept 'no-thing' or 'nothingness'. Therefore Saraha says: Things and no-things fetter Buddhahood. As long as there is subject and object, there is the world (of subjective interpretation). The statement 'there is neither subject nor object' is a conceptualization and hence 'memory' and the world (of subjective interpretation). The non-conceptualizable reality of what there is, is (their) self-sameness. 'Self-sameness, self-sameness' is a mere concept, hence Saraha exclaims: Without making a difference between world and self-sameness.

"Genuine, quiet spontaneity cannot be conceptualized. Conceptualization is 'memory' because it is subjectively relating mind. When this 'memory' has disappeared like mist, Saraha's words apply: Let the genuine subject stay alone, o yogi!

"But if one hankers after this non-memory, it is like a drop of oil floating on water, because there are still propositions entertained. But when all attributes have subsided in the absolutely real, then, as Saraha says: Know this to be like water poured into water."

The image of water being poured into water does not mean that the subject is absorbed in something greater than itself. Apart from conceptualizing a peak experience, it denies the very fact of knowledge. All that this image intends is the unitive character of the experience: "In the same way as water poured into water cannot be separated, so appearance and openness are to be known as indivisible", says Karma Phrin-las-pa.[161] With this interpretation he restates the metaphysical and ontological nature of Tantrism. There is no world other than the world of appearance, but it is not 'nothing but appearance', the view of the various, intrinsically negative, transcendentalisms.

The Goal is to Be

Ordinarily, it seems, we are beset with an urge for bifurcation, and the first emergence of a possible sense of I-ness is marked by hostility, resentment, acrimony. Subsequently, everything is set in a strange love-hate ambiguity, deriving from the initial hostility. The integral personality is severed into a mind and a body, difficult to reunite. Beyond the individual, the whole universe is divided into appearance and reality. Our reactions to the world around us are no less divided; we speak of Saṃsāra and Nirvāṇa, of relative truth and absolute truth, and when these ideas become dominant, our attitudes become ever more rigid, and finally the two poles become incompatible. The ensuing conflict becomes unbearable and we try to find a way out, but since the bifurcation contains a hidden evaluation so that mind is more valuable than the body, Nirvāṇa superior to Saṃsāra, to say nothing of the alleged contrast between reality and appearance, we unwittingly side with what seems to be more valuable and, by attending to the more valued pole, through what is commonly called 'meditation', we merely perpetuate the bifurcation and the conflict. Saraha is quite outspoken when he says:

> "By the swindle of meditation freedom is not found";

and gNyis-med Avadhūtipa elaborates this dictum by stating:[162]

> "Some people say that freedom is found when one holds steady the proper understanding of the noetic (moment) that comes in the wake of a deeper insight, after one has composed oneself. Not knowing that (Being) is for ever in a state of composure, they do not find liberation by this imaginary composure."

The last sentence of this quotation emphasizes the importance of looking for the integral personality, and of tearing away what prevents us from being. The goal of Tantrism is *to be*, and the way to it may be called a process of self-actualization. However, it is extremely important not to be mistaken about the term 'self', which in a subjectivistic context is the excuse for any oddity that might pop into one's head. The self is never an idiosyncrasy, it is not even an entity, but a convention to point to the subject character of man as man, but not of man as this or that particular individual with these or those particular traits. If the goal is to be, and if we let 'self' stand for the way it feels to be, there is a hidden premise in this: the determining self (which makes us feel to be a self) must be a possible self. It must represent a set of authentic potentialities of the individual and must be a self whose realization lies within the realm of genuine possibility. This fact has constantly been forgotten in the course of the history of philosophy, and the solution of the problem of man's Being has been attempted by either belittling or aggrandizing man. The former attempt is the well-known Kantian assumption of the twofold nature of man, a godlike noumenal self of man and his merely human self. The godlike self is an image that man forms of himself as an 'idealized person' which is then identified with man's 'real self' and so becomes the perspective from which he views himself and discovers that his everyday life self, his phenomenal self, falls remarkably short of the imaginary and postulated qualities of the supposedly real self. The latter attempt begins with the deification of one isolated individual, which reduces all other individuals to inferior beings, and finds its climax in the deification of the theoretical ego as the Supreme Being, which, of course, excludes the possibility that any human being can really be. If the self is a superhuman self, like Kant's transcendental ego, or Hegel's world spirit, or the Hinduist Ātman, man cannot become such an impossibility. Such a postulated self, whatever name it may be given and however much man may try to identify himself with it in his imagination, is a pseudo-self, a self impossible of realization. The arrogance inherent in every form of deification merely serves to perpetuate the dualization of man and initiates a destructive conflict that spreads within and without. The impossible attempt to identify oneself with an impossibility only leads to self-deception, which immerses man deeper and deeper in his own fictions, so aptly illustrated in the texts by the simile of the silk-worm in its cocoon.[163]

Tantrism does not ask man to turn himself into an impossibility, but to realize his potentialities. The *Āhapramāṇa-samyak-nāma-ḍākinī-upadeśa* declares:[164]

> "As the seed, so the tree—
> As the tree, so the fruit.
> Looking at the whole world in this way—
> This then is relativity."

This aphorism not only underlines the fact that the goal is a possible goal, it also recognizes the fact that all that is is relative and so not only re-emphasizes possibility but also avoids the speculative slip into the absolutization of some particular existent. Padma dkar-po's commentary on the above aphorism is extremely significant and, together with the passages he quotes in support of his interpretation and the commentaries on these passages by gNyis-med Avadhūtipa and Karma Phrin-las-pa, reveals the depth of Tantric thought. Padma dkar-po's words are:[165]

> "In the same way as the existential presence of mind, in its indivisibility of profundity and radiancy, is the seed, so the tree of mind as the unity of Saṃsāra and Nirvāṇa grows as the path, and according to (the nature of) this tree there ripens its fruit Mahāmudrā, which is Dharmakāya, the unity of the Two Truths[166] that by themselves are not a duality. In the *Dohās* it is said:
>
> The perfect tree of unitary mind
> Has grown all over the three worlds.
> Its flower, compassion, bears the fruit 'being-for-others'.
> Its name is 'most excellent for-otherness'.
>
> and:
>
> The perfect tree—the open dimension of Being, is in full bloom,
> And its blossoms are the many forms of compassion.

Its later fruit comes quite spontaneously,
And the bliss is not some other mind.

Although at the outset, Mind-as-such, due to its (function as either intrinsic awareness or unknowing) appears divided into Saṃsāra and Nirvāṇa, it should be attended to on the path in such a way as having never parted from its unitary presence. In so doing the fruit is realized as being one:

One seed grows two stems,
But the fruit is identical with the seed.
He who is aware of indivisibility
Is freed from Saṃsāra and Nirvāṇa.

Similarly, Nāgārjuna says in his *Dharmadhātustotra:*

From all seeds
Fruits similar to their cause grow.
Which intelligent person can claim
A fruit without a seed?
The 'field' (Tathāgatagarbha) as the seed
Is the bearer of all qualities.

In the *Guhyasamājatantra*[167] we read:

Ah, the continuity of Saṃsāra; ah, sublime Nirvāṇa.

And in the *Hevajra*:

Saṃsāra purified, with no infatuation left,
Becomes Nirvāṇa.

And Vajrahṛdaya declared:

From the seed of pure compassion
Planted in the field of man
Grows the Wish-Fulfilling Tree
Of the open dimension of Being.
There is no doubt that
Through the intention of all beings
From this Wish-Fulfilling Tree
The fruit of pure spirituality will grow."

In speaking of the profundity and radiancy of mind, Padma dkar-po at once draws our attention away from the shallowness of conceptual thought and the dullness of its systematizations and directs it to the source from which both insight (knowledge) and opinion (unknowing) may develop, their development being the way in which we deal with ourselves as representing a certain problem situation. Significantly, he speaks of the unity of Saṃsāra and Nirvāṇa, which are terms for judgments of perception rather than concrete entities. Saṃsāra is a problem situation which prompts us to find a solution, but the solution we find is just another problem situation, and to replace Saṃsāra by Nirvāṇa is rankest escapism, as frustrating as Saṃsāra's rat-race. This realization finds its expression in the statement that Nirvāṇa is just as much a quagmire as is Saṃsāra. The conclusion to be drawn is that problems are not solved, but dissolve, and the dissolution of one problem entails that of another. Saraha indicates this in the words:

> "Just as in utter darkness (all darkness is dispelled)
> When the moonstone spreads its light,
> In a single moment of unsurpassable bliss supreme
> All the evils of judgments are vanquished."

gNyis-med-Avadhūtipa elaborates these words as follows:[168]

> "The obscurations formed by emotions and by the intellectual fog are like utter darkness; instruction given by the genuine teacher who is like the moonstone vanquishing all darkness, makes understood what has not been understood, hence 'Just as in utter darkness. . . .' In the same way as the moonstone need not carry the darkness from one place to another, so also the emotions and the intellectual fog need not be rejected. Hence 'spreads its light'. Simultaneously with pointing out the unusual bliss supreme, which is not sullied by the dirt of Saṃsāra and by the dirt of Nirvāṇa, the intentionality of Buddhahood is seen, hence 'In a single moment. . . .' Conceptualizing is the evil of judging, non-conceptualization is the happiness of concentration. Since by knowing the fictions of 'memory' to be mind-exhausting, and by enjoying 'non-memory', the conceptualizing mind is conquered, (Saraha says): 'All the evils. . . .' "

The fact that problems are not solved but dissolve or, to state it otherwise, that man outgrows them by developing insight rather than by developing fictions, is discussed again in connection with meditation which, more often than not, fixes the mind on some object in relationship to the meditating subject, and then merely strengthens the subjectivism that has been felt to be so frustrating:

> "Get rid of the fetter that consists in the division
> Between what is to be meditated upon and who meditates.
> One has always been free!
> Do not be fooled by the I and the other,"

says Saraha, and Karma Phrin-las-pa remarks:[169]

> "It may be argued that if I am free, the other may still be someone to be freed. The answer is that when I become free, the self-appearance (of self) has passed and there is nothing left of an other-appearance. Therefore there is no being that as someone else has to be freed. To give an example, we may dream that we suffer together with many others, but when we wake up we have become free from our suffering in the dream and there is no other being that has to be freed from his suffering in the dream."

The 'I' and the 'other' are concepts and belong to the conceptualizing activity of the mind, which by its conceptualization denies freedom as an existential value. It 'imagines' freedom and abrogates this imaginary freedom to the equally imaginary self or ego, not realizing that 'ego' or 'I' is but an index word indicating the speaker, not some entity within or above the person who pronounces this word. Only in this fictional world of the ego can the question of the other occur, and such subjectivism is fraught with danger. The individual may be genuinely concerned with gaining freedom, but he may be equally obsessed by the idea of freedom in a mis-directed way. He will then try to impose this idea on others, and his fanaticism to 'liberate' the rest of mankind knows no bounds. What he calls liberation is total enslavement.

The dream is a particularly apt illustration of the fallaciousness of both the ego-sense and the subjectivism that goes with it. 'To wake up' is the literal translation of the root *budh* from which the word Buddha, 'he who has woken up' is derived. When we wake up, what has happened to our dream-ego? Precisely the same that has happened to the *other*-images: they have dissolved. This dissolution is the recognition of the latent possibility having become the overt actuality, termed Mahāmudrā in view of its impressiveness, or Dharmakāya in view of its existential reality and value, or the unity of the Two Truths, by which is meant that while Awareness is the basic existential fact, it is never anything else but the images through which it manifests itself. Again, it is significant that one speaks of two truths. Unless one absolutizes and thereby falsifies truth, truth does not and can never lie exclusively on one side or the other, not somewhere betwixt and between, but only in a wider perspective that incorporates and unites both.

In support of his thesis Padma dkar-po quotes two verses by Saraha. These contain the essence, not only of Buddhism in general but also of Buddhist Tantrism in particular; its two key-terms are 'compassion' and 'open dimension of Being' which, as we have seen, is a term reflecting back from the 'content' of the perception to the perception itself. According to Karma Phrin-las-pa these two verses reveal their specific meaning when taken together with the one preceding them in Saraha's work:

> "All (the beings) are the continuously present Buddha;
> Since mind is intrinsically pure,
> It, indeed, is the stainless, sublime citadel."

This verse re-emphasizes the basic fact of Awareness and Being as coterminous, and gNyis-med Avadhūtipa in his commentary elaborates this fact. He says:[170]

> "The sentient beings of the three worlds without exception are not separate from the intentionality (meaningfulness) of Buddhahood, hence 'All (the beings). . . .' Although different names are given to it such as 'sentient being' when mind is impure, and 'Buddha' when mind has become pure in itself, Mind-as-such has nothing to do with origination and so on. Since mind is radiant in itself, Saraha says: 'Since mind. . . .' However, the very attribute 'mind' is a defilement (i.e., we have a concept and confuse the concept with the reality for which the concept stands). Therefore, (Mind-as-such) is free from such notions as mind or no-mind, and need not be freed from them, as Saraha indicates: 'It, indeed. . . .' "

Here, the ontological fact of Mind-as-such is clearly brought out by contrasting it with the postulated mind of subjective speculation. Karma Phrin-las-pa's explanation goes even deeper. He brings out both the metaphysical and mystical character of Buddhism. Mysticism is a definite kind of experience which is both a way of knowledge and a state of consciousness; it has nothing to do with mystification or an other-worldliness that carries with it a nebulous outlook on the world we live in; metaphysics is the attempt to tell us how to get the things of *this* world into perspective; it is not the ability to reveal truths about a world which lies beyond the reach of the senses of ordinary mortals and hence nowhere. But while the metaphysician attempts to give a general description of his perspective, the mystic speaks of an individual occurrence. Thus the metaphysician speaks of Dharmadhātu 'the dimension of Being', the mystic of Dharmakāya, 'the existential experience of Being'. Both understand by 'Being' an absoluteness that is not relativated to the relativity of all that is. Absoluteness has not 'come into existence' and therefore also cannot 'go out of existence'; figuratively speaking, it 'continues', it is not subject to time, but encompasses time as a possible interpretation. So, Karma Phrin-las-pa says:[171]

> "All sentient beings possess the nature of Buddhahood, continuously present since its beginningless beginning. What is this nature of Buddhahood? It is the existential fact and presence of mind; since it is intrinsically pure, (it is) the beginningless time-encompassing dimension of Being (Dharmadhātu) unbroken, impartial, radiant in itself, as the pristine existential experience of Being (Dharmakāya). Is this the natural potentiality (of man)? Yes. Since beginningless time the actuality of mind has been present in purity, and when it is pure without the slightest trace of dualizing concepts which are but incidental blemishes, it is said to be the arrival at the citadel of sublime enlightenment of double purity."

It is in the light of Being that Saraha's subsequent verses must be interpreted, especially since all commentators agree that in them Dharmakāya and Sambhogakāya are referred to in their practical application, because here they are a matter of lived experience, which involves man's behaviour towards and in the world surrounding him.

But nowhere has the search for values relevant to man's existence been so much falsified as in the norms, ideals, duties, that have been set up without a grounding in the realities of life. Utilitarianism, emotivism, compromises with urgencies, subjectivistic evaluations, demands of 'society' or 'morality', commands of a transcendental deity, all indicate their intellectualistic irrelevance. What are we to make of being told, on the one hand, 'Thou shalt not kill' but, on the other hand, when someone takes this admonition seriously and refuses to be turned into a common killer, he is put into jail?

The ethical principle in Tantrism is termed 'compassion' and is based on the recognition of the fact that everything that is, has by virtue of its being, its value. There is nothing in the world that is not valuable. The ethical principle involves both value-judgment and application of the judgment. The value-judgment has to take into account two factors: (*a*) the value of what there is by virtue of its being, and (*b*) the value of each particular instant of what there is and related to other particular instants of what there is. While all that is is 'eternally good' because of the fact that it *is*, it is 'temporally good' as representing a certain condition or state of Being. 'Eternally good' is the all-embracing open dimension of Being, 'temporally good' are the transitory manifestations of and in it. From this it follows that evil arises when we treat the transitory manifestations as something other than what they actually are, when we elevate them into an eternal principle. To exemplify: determinate pleasures exist only under certain circumstances, but never under all circumstances. The assumption that they hold under all circumstances defeats its own purpose by causing us to become irritated when the specific pleasures are not present, which adds to the unpleasantness we experience at the moment. Similarly, sexual passion is good as long as it is recognized as a transitory phenomenon, but if it is treated as the sole end of human existence it fails to yield its goodness. Instead, it increases frustration. With the compulsive collector of physical contacts it is likewise with a drunkard: he cannot stop, does not want to stop, cannot think of anything else, and can never have enough.

Another point to note in connection with value-judgment is that there cannot be a negative judgment in the sense that something is being deprived of its value. Value-negation can only be understood as the negation of this or that particular value as inappropriate to this or that particular object. Appearance is good in its playfulness and the fascination that goes with its images, but it is evil in the sense that it fails to give the satisfaction that is expected of it and which, because we fail to recognize appearance as what it is, it cannot give.

The ethical principle demands the recognition of what there is as the bearer of a value that constitutes its existence; when this recognition is absent it becomes opinionatedness and the morality rooted in it is mere superstition, which it attempts to conceal by authoritarianism. However, it is not enough to recognize the value; it is important for the individual, in order that he may enjoy a meaningful life, to apply this value-judgment in his dealing with whatever he encounters. This implies that the individual has to act responsibly and meaningfully, not purposively in subjectivistic misjudgment. This acting responsibly is indicated by the term 'for-otherness' which is said to be the maturation of 'compassion'. We must distinguish compassion as responsible action—the word *karuṇā* is derived from the root *kṛ* 'to act'—from sentimentality with its mercantilism and utter lack of understanding of the human situation. In sentimentality, which poses as 'being-for-others', the other has no value at all except that he is a means to self-gratification. The words of this mercantile self-gratification may have changed, but there is no change in behaviour. Once it was "And when thou dost alms let not thy left hand know what thy right hand doth. That thy alms be in secret: and thy Father who seeth in secret will repay thee". Today it is: "Your charitable donation is tax-deductible." How little the other counts is borne out by the fact that these 'philanthropic' despisers of mankind rarely speak of individuals, but mostly of achieving a target. Compassion, by contrast, recognizes the being of the other, it does not deprive him of his value (it does not throw him into the gutter first, so to speak, so that later in pulling him out I can self-gratifyingly say: Look how much I have done for you), but it starts from his values and helps him to develop himself. To act compassionately is not to be overwhelmed by an emotion, but is always to act feelingly and knowingly. Compassionate action is, in Saraha's words, the flowering of the existential awareness of Being (Dharmakāya) which bears the fruit of 'being-for-others'. This means that out of this awareness we cannot but act compassionately. In its existential context this flowering is technically known as Sambhogakāya, 'empathetic being'. In simplest terms of cognition, empathy is the perception of an object in terms of its movement or its tendency to move, whether actual or supposed. The object is not merely noted cognitively but it is 'felt' to be. A tree, for instance, is not merely seen as a member of its class, but it is 'felt' swaying in the wind. The object is thereby experienced in a new light. It becomes the guide, while the self submits to its lead so that a more intimate and lively appreciation of the object is achieved. This involves imagination and feeling which are brought to prominence by empathy. Through empathetic perception the subject is able to attain in his own being the fullest possible apprehension of the object's intrinsic value and being. Through this ability to see more and more aspects of the many-sidedness of a person or even a thing, the perceiver and the perceived become more like each other as they both move toward unity, which has a special flavour of perfection, aliveness, finality and bliss. Karma Phrin-las-pa[172] indicates this movement toward unity and bliss in commenting on Saraha's second verse in Padma dkar-po's explanation of the passage from the *Āhapramāṇa-samyak-nāma-ḍākinī-upadeśa*:

> "At the stage of the path, by experiencing the unity of the tree of understanding all that is as (partaking in) the open dimension of Being, and its full-blown flower of absolute compassion, there comes the awakening to an existential value-being awareness (*Dharmakāya*) that is not tied either to worldliness or to quiescence; and (this awareness) exhibits the two *Rūpakāyas* as as many patterns as are

appropriate to those who have to be guided, by virtue of one's being having been cultivated by many forms of compassion. These three existential value-patterns (*Dharmakāya* and the two *Rūpakāyas*) have been present in their spontaneity all the time, their later fruit is the *Svābhāvikakāya* or *Mahāsukhakāya*.[173] That which in its self-manifestation appears as Buddha-existence is not an appearance other than that of mind, and it is also not an appearance of a mind that is different from one's Being."

Similarly gNyis-med Avadhūtipa says:[174]

"Since this comes effortlessly, it is spontaneous. First there is 'memory' as the cause and then 'non-memory' as the effect. Then 'non-memory' becomes the cause and 'un-origination' is the effect. Then 'un-originatedness' is the cause and 'what transcends the intellect' is the effect."

Empathetic perception presupposes the presence of existential values which can be 'felt' as belonging intimately to oneself. This presence is Being-as-such in terms of metaphysics and Mind-as-such in terms of our being aware of Being-as-such, while in its felt existentiality it is *Dharmakāya*, beyond the intellect in the sense that it makes the intellect and its operations possible but is not caught in its fictions, which come into existence and also fade out of it. In the same way as Being-as-such cannot be reduced to some kind of being (nor hypostatized or deified into some other kind of being), so also Mind-as-such is irreducible, and the judgments we make are the ways through which it manifests itself to us and in this self-manifestation gives us a chance to 'let things be'. In commenting on Saraha's verses stating that one seed bears an identical fruit in spite of growing two stems, gNyis-med Avadhūtipa says:[175]

"Although out of that which is beyond the intellect and does not come into existence, 'memory' and 'non-memory' arise, Mind-as-such remains unoriginated. Out of it Saṃsāra and Nirvāṇa appear as a duality, or as Saraha states: 'One seed grows two stems.' The *Dharmakāya*, which is beyond the intellect, is not a different fruit, hence Saraha continues: 'But the fruit is identical with the seed.'

Moreover, while (Mind-as-such) is the cause of Saṃsāra and also the cause of Nirvāṇa, Saraha uses the expression: 'He who is aware of indivisibility'. A low-level yogi is concerned with freedom from the one-sidedness of Saṃsāra, a medium-level yogi with freedom from mere Nirvāṇa, but the high-level yogi's understanding consists in the fact that he neither rejects nor accepts (i.e., identifies himself with) the fictions that stem from a mind immersed in Saṃsāra; that he neither rejects nor accepts a state of quiescence, which is a mind that has passed into Nirvāṇa. Since Saṃsāra is not an entity in itself, he is not afraid of it, and since Nirvāṇa is not found as an entity in itself, either, he does not hope for it. This is the way of the yogis, and so Saraha concludes: 'Is freed from Saṃsāra and Nirvāṇa.' "

Hope and fear are here said to inhibit, if not to destroy, the capacity to perceive and to act. Both hope and fear assume that Saṃsāra and Nirvāṇa are real objects located in some place; they blur the understanding that Saṃsāra and Nirvāṇa are interpretations, ways of trying to make sense of, and to come to terms with, the world in which man lives and of which he is a part. But interpretations in terms of Saṃsāra and Nirvāṇa fail because of the hidden assumption that they are objects to be feared or to be hoped for. To understand that fear of Saṃsāra and hope for Nirvāṇa are both unfounded is not to explain Saṃsāra and Nirvāṇa away, but is to reveal the dimension that underlies these two limiting judgments. This dimension is likened to 'celestial space', the term *ākāśa* (*nam-mkha'*) indicating both 'sky' and 'space'. The point to note here is that space must not be understood as being 'some thing'. It has no qualities as such and any attribute used in connection with it is only meant to emphasize its quality-less-ness. Space extends 'as far as this world' which is all that is. Space must also not be understood as 'empty space'. On the one hand, space would have been qualified as '*something* empty', and, on the other hand, when there is something there is no space. Space is just a term for the fact that the world is 'extended' in its plurality, each individual being distant from other individual beings, but all of them 'filling' the world as space. Space cannot be separated or abstracted from Being-as-such, and the individual beings are not *in* space, which would make space something beyond or outside them and even outside Being. As an experience of a 'creative openness' encompassing and, as it were, bringing this world into existence, space is a most suitable simile for the 'goal' experience in its vividness, for the feeling of really being and for the value of being, while as 'sky' it indicates the luminousness and openness as well as the creativeness of the experience, just as clouds arise and disappear in it. It is for these reasons that the word 'sky' or 'space' is used to refer to the goal-experience, of which Saraha says:

"A 1 The longer one looks at the sky clear from its beginning,
The more one ceases to see it as something.
When just-so-ness (is present, all else) ceases.
2 The fool is deceived by his error about the natural mind,
And all the beings refute each other, but
Are unable to point out the real because of their arrogance.
3 The whole world is infatuated with meditation
4 But nobody can point out the genuine.

B The root of mind cannot be shown.
Because of the three kinds of togetherness
Wherever it rises, wherever it sinks, and
Wherever it stays, it is not known clearly.
For him who understands this rootlessness
It suffices to receive the Guru's instruction.

C 'The actuality of Saṃsāra is the reality of Mind'—
Know this to be the words of Saraha to the deluded.
Although the genuine cannot be expressed in words
It can be seen by the eye of the teacher's instruction.
When good and evil alike have been eaten,
Not the slightest flaw remains."

While gNyis-med Avadhūtipa considers these verses as descriptive of the goal, Karma Phrin-las-pa understands them as referring to the removal of the wrong notions during the traversing of the Path. Both authors agree in rejecting any concretization of the experience. gNyis-med Avadhūtipa says:[176]

"The fact that the goal which is beyond hope and fear cannot be shown (concretely) is illustrated by the simile of 'sky-space'. Space is not affected by any such propositional statements as existence or non-existence. 'Space' is a word in use. Since it is not a 'something' it does not generalize (distinct) feelings as is the case when forms are seen and when thereby a distinct feeling-judgment occurs. Since space is not affected by origination or cessation, Saraha says: 'The sky clear from its beginning'. Mind-as-such, when looked at, with no conditions (distorting its serenity), is known as 'non-memory'; when looked at again as 'unoriginatedness' and when looked at once again as 'unattainable by the intellect'. Hence Saraha says: 'The longer one looks, the more one ceases to see it as something'. By understanding this as the goal or *Dharmakāya*, the knowing and the knowable cease (as a duality), as Saraha says: 'When just-so-ness (is present, all else) ceases'. But when one does not understand this just-so-ness which is together with all that is as not concretizable, and thinks that concretization is the goal, *Dharmakāya*, Saraha points out: 'The fool is deceived by his error about the natural mind.' If the sentient beings of the three worlds think and ponder that they have to get rid of their emotional obscurations, Saraha says: 'And all the beings refute each other.' First overcome by emotions and then overcome by intellectualism, they are like a recaptured escapee from prison. Their arrogance does not realize that just-so-ness submerges in what is beyond the intellect. Hence Saraha's words: 'Are unable to point out the real because of their arrogance.'

"Since all beings in the triple world do not understand that meditation is to let be, Saraha says: 'The whole world is infatuated with meditation.' The yogi's understanding (fusing with) the absolutely real, pure in itself and free from all propositions about is, cannot be pointed out by similes or the thing itself. Since an intellectual fiction cannot understand it, Saraha says: 'But nobody can point out the genuine.' The root of all that is, is mind, but mind is not found as something in itself. Since its root cannot be shown, Saraha states: 'The root of mind cannot be shown'.

"That which appears as stemming from mind, comes from 'non-memory', stays in 'non-memory', and subsides in 'non-memory'. This togetherness with appearance is experienceable in 'non-memory'. Mind, as long as it is not distorted by conditions, is 'non-memory' and this is (its) openness, which rises from 'unorigination', stays there and subsides in it. This togetherness with openness is experienceable in 'unorigination'. Mind-as-such, as long as memory and non-memory do not rise, is beyond origination and cessation, and since it is beyond the realm of the intellect, the absolutely real rises from, stays in, and subsides in what is the essence of the three aspects of time. When one understands the togetherness with unorigination as being unimaginable, Saraha's words are: 'Because of the three kinds of togetherness'.

"When one understands mind, then appearance, openness, and unorigination cease the moment they appear, as Saraha indicates: 'Wherever it rises, wherever it sinks'.

"And since one does not find the absolutely real by searching for it, Saraha says: 'Wherever it stays, it is not known clearly'. Since there is no root for (the fiction) of 'sentient beings', there is also no root for the awareness of 'Buddha'. This rootlessness is the root of enlightenment. Since it is not objectifiable, Saraha declares: 'For him who understands this rootlessness'.

"When one understands the nature of enlightenment, simultaneously with the instruction in togetherness by the Guru, there is neither 'memory' nor 'oblivion'. Hence Saraha states: 'It suffices to receive the Guru's instruction'.

"If one says that it suffices to call Saṃsāra Saṃsāra, one should bear in mind that there is Saṃsāra when one does not know the actuality of mind. In the same way as pleasures

XIII. Green Tārā [green: colour of overcoming difficulties] (*Author's collection*)

XIV. Uṣṇīṣavijayā. Symbol of supreme Buddha-awareness (*Author's collection*)

and sorrows in a dream are nothing else but mental events and (in the same way as) the waking awareness, the dreaming of a dream and the dream awareness are not different (from each other) in their unoriginatedness, so also the mental processes (summarized by) 'memory' and mind (as) 'non-memory' and Mind-as-such (as) unoriginatedness are not different (from each other). Since Saṃsāra and Nirvāṇa are the enticing performances of Mind-as-such unborn, Saraha declares: 'The actuality of Saṃsāra is the reality of Mind'.

"Since people dismiss the knowledge of the actuality of mind by various means, Saraha continues: 'Know this to be the words of Saraha to the deluded'.

"The yogic understanding is genuineness. This just-so-ness is unattainable by intellectual means and cannot be expressed in words. 'Memory' comes from what can be expressed in words, but this unitary awareness cannot be expressed in words, and hence 'memory' does not arise. As Saraha says: 'Although the genuine cannot be expressed in words.' The absolutely real can be seen by the pure eye of original awareness, opened by the true Guru; as Saraha states: 'It can be seen by the eye of the teacher's instruction'.

"When it is understood in this way, the knowing and the knowable are both consumed, what can one still say of positive and negative aspects? Saraha declares: 'When good and evil alike have been eaten'.

"If someone were to ask whether good is helpful and evil detrimental, the answer would have to be that nothing of this sort obtains. As Saraha sums up: 'Not the slightest flaw remains'. "

gNyis-med Avadhūtipa's slightly technical commentary elucidates many points that are important for what is involved in Tantrism as a means to change our view of ourselves as well as of the world around us and, with this change of view, also to alter our attitudes. First of all, he explains the transition from categorical perception to aesthetic or intrinsic perception. Usually, when we perceive something, certain mnemic traces left by past experiences are excited and these, in turn, arouse certain emotions and bodily adjustments and feelings. These 'mnemic consequences', to use a term by C. D. Broad,[177] not only co-exist with the apprehension of what is perceived, but enter into a specific kind of relationship to it, giving the perceptual situation its specific external reference. But when no traces are excited, the external reference not only will be very vague, it may even be non-existent. Ordinary perception, which relates what we perceive to our needs, fears, and interests, is fatiguing and frustrating because we abstract and thereby fail to perceive other aspects of the perceived object. In this sense, ordinary perception is falsification and a habitual perpetration of falsities. On the other hand, to perceive intrinsically is to be much more alert, to be much more astute and penetrating. Rather than detracting from action it makes action much more appropriate to the situation. Only when the mind is 'fixed' on some aspect, commonly referred to as meditation or pure contemplation, action becomes inhibited and all feeling retrogressive. In such contemplation, all spontaneity and naturalness is lost. Intrinsic perception is both active and passive; it is passive in letting things be, in not forcing itself upon them, and it is active in being itself more alert. It is a broadening of the perceptual field, as vast as the sky or space which is the whole world.

The mind is never anywhere else but in its functioning which is its self-manifestation as mental events (*sems-las byung-ba*). These events are directly interrelated in a characteristic way and stand in a common asymmetrical relation to something, in the sense that each of these events is a constituent in the *fact* that they are all related to each other in this characteristic way. This fact, standing in a common asymmetrical relation to all the mental events, is termed mind (*sems*) which is not an *existent* centre but only a *subsistent* centre. But even to talk of a *subsistent* centre is to concretize the free functioning of what, even at the risk of conceptualization, can only be referred to as Mind-as-such (*sems-nyid*). Analytically speaking, appearance is always together with openness, and openness is always together with unoriginatedness which, in turn, is always together with what cannot be grasped intellectually. This is the 'rootlessness' of both the Buddha-awareness and of the categorical perception of ordinary beings, because if something is rooted in something it has been concretized and reduced to some construct of the mind. The statement that Saṃsāra and Nirvāṇa are performances of Mind-as-such means that the mind is composed of its objects interrelated in certain particular ways (Saṃsāra, Nirvāṇa). The Saṃsāric or Nirvāṇic mind is simply the fact that a certain set of objects (Saṃsāra, Nirvāṇa) are related to each other in a certain way at a certain moment. Hence the famous statement: 'In a moment a sentient (Saṃsāric) being, in a moment a Buddha.' And a certain mental event ('memory') is simply the fact that a certain object (Saṃsāra) stands in certain relation to certain other interrelated objects (Nirvāṇa) at a certain moment. The important consequence of this conception is that Buddhahood is not something outside this world or outside the reach of the mind, and, since the mind 'embodies' itself, Buddhahood can be realized 'in this body'. As ordinary beings we see ourselves and the world from a self-centred and selfish point of view and judge whatever we encounter as good or evil to the extent that it promotes or obstructs our selfish interests. As Buddhas we see the world whole and unified, and reality is seen more clearly. The source of our growth or our stagnation lies within us, and to be in a state of Being is neither ruled by laws of outer-reality (Saṃsāra) nor by inner-psychic laws (Nirvāṇa); it means rather to be in both simultaneously. Since Buddhahood is in *this* world and in *this* body, it is life-validating, it makes life worth while, and to the extent that we are able to see the world whole and as a unity there is nothing that we have to be afraid of, because fear is related to the ego, and there also is nothing to hope for, because all hopes have been fulfilled.

Karma Phrin-las-pa, who interprets Saraha's verses as implying the removal of misconceptions on the path, sub-divides them as indicated. The first part (A) is meant to get rid of the urge to cling to the experience of radiancy and openness which in (1) is described in general terms, while in (2) it is pointed out that persons, in their arrogance they display by holding to dogmatic formulations, are unable to understand the existential presence of Being, and in (3) it is shown that meditation, as practised by a 'deluded' person who fixes his mind on something and therefore is unable to perceive anything else and merely impoverishes himself, is equally incapable to grasp Being, and in (4) a summary is given. The second part (B) deals with the rejection of adherence to a specific procedure, and the third part (C) indicates the use of symbols pointing to Being-as-such. He also adduces interpretations by other scholars. The fact that different interpretations are possible shows the stimulating force of Saraha's thought, and also emphasizes the fact that Tantrism is not a system with ready-made answers. Karma Phrin-las-pa's words are:[178]

(A1) "When there is the urge to cling to the specific experience of radiancy and openness, this experience itself must be (experienced) as follows: When one looks with the eye of original awareness at Mind-as-such, pure from the beginning, genuine and spontaneous, like the sky, (its) understanding grows ever more firm while appearance grows ever more weak. When by looking repeatedly (in this way) (the understanding) has become absolutely firm, the seeing which believes in the concrete existence (of what is perceived) ceases by itself. If someone asks whether such radiancy and openness (clear) as the sky ever ceases, the answer is that when the understanding is firm without there being a concentration or post-concentration state, all delusive appearances ceases. In this context Lama Bal-po says: 'When "memory" looks at "unoriginatedness", the vision of what is beyond the intellect ceases,' and Par-phu-ba says: 'The sky pure in itself from its beginning is nothing to be seen, but by looking at it, seeing it (as something) ceases.' Both (Lamas) refer merely to openness. Rang-byung rdo-rje declares: 'When one looks at the concept with the concept that "mind-as-such is pure from its beginning", one may come to know its fictional character, but since there is still the belief in its fictional character, this, too, has to be got rid of. To illustrate this point: if one looks at the sky, all other seeing may cease, but the belief in (what is perceived) has not yet ceased.' Rang-byung rdo-rje combines his interpretation with (Saraha's subsequent line) 'The fool is deceived by his error about the natural mind' due to the fact that (in attending merely to mind) compassion stops. He thus speaks from the viewpoint of radiancy. However, both interpretations are not mutually contradictory. The basic text (by Saraha) presents their unity.

(A2) "The natural mind is genuine (subject-)mind (*yid*). The fools in their ignorance deceive themselves by not knowing (what) meditation is and by pondering over an artificially set-up content, and thus create an obstacle to an understanding of the existential presence of Being-as-such. Because of this all the individuals that pursue a certain path disapprove of each other and in their arrogance about their own philosophical tenets or practices look down on others (saying): 'This is not to be practised', 'This is plain nonsense'. Since just-so-ness cannot be shown thereby, this (arrogance) has to be discarded.

(A3) "Without relying on the helpfulness of the true Guru, (the followers of) a wordly meditation only concentrate on nothingness or quiescence, and they all become deluded by the spiritual darkness (of such) meditation and do not see the real and clear pristine awareness.

(A4) "Therefore, nobody who merely listens, ponders, and conceptualizes can realize the existential presence of Being, genuine in itself.

(B) "The root of mind or the primordial just-so-ness cannot be shown (as something). How is this (to be understood)? Through the three kinds of togetherness, i.e., the body (is) the togetherness of appearance and openness, speech (is) the togetherness of sound and openness; and mind (is) the togetherness of intrinsic perception and openness. Or, (another explanation is that) appearance and openness are together, openness and unoriginatedness are together, unoriginatedness and what is beyond the intellect are together. Because of this, one does not find the root of these three kinds of togetherness by looking for the root from where they have grown, just as one does not find the root of the togetherness of fire and heat, water and moistness. Since one cannot concretize (this togetherness) nor recognize determinate characteristics (of it) even if one investigates the origin, end, and presence (of this togetherness), all that is must be understood as being 'rootless' and 'groundless'. He who thinks of and understands just-so-ness as having no root, will destroy all imputations from within when he relies on the instruction by the Guru who makes him understand that the rootlessness of conceptual thought is Mind-as-such; and when he has no more doubts, he should let it suffice. If there is the urge to cling to a specific method, try to experience openness as having no root.

(C) "All that is subsumed under Saṃsāra and Nirvāṇa, i.e., what appears on the part of deviation is 'concrete' Saṃsāra, and what appears on the part of pristine awareness as 'not-quite-so concrete' Nirvāṇa, is the reality of Mind with no propositions about it. Know that Saraha has repeatedly told this to the deluded people. The genuine presence of Being-as-such cannot be shown or captured in words, but it can be seen by the eye of pristine awareness experienceable individually through the symbols and instruction by a teacher. Since there is no place and no chance to implant traces (of a limiting experience) in this vision of Being-as-such when what belongs to Saṃsāra and to Nirvāṇa has been eaten alike as having the same flavour, there is not the slightest chance that the evil (of a limiting experience) will mature."

In contrasting Lama Bal-po and Par-phu-ba with Rang-byung rdo-rje, Karma Phrin-las-pa points to what may be called a danger in effecting a change of perspective. Although intrinsic perception is felt to be more worth while than categorical perception, the intention of intrinsic perception is not that we should be lost in the vision of the openness of Being, but rather that we should act, which is to radiate life. But the one aspect is not possible without the other. If we try to 'fix' the openness of Being, reducing it to a conceptual content of the ego-centred mind, the light, quite literally, 'goes out' and we are engulfed in a self-deceptive darkness, which we haughtily judge as the last word to be said about anything.

We are with our body, our speech, and our mind, simply as that; it is by attempting to explain Being as deriving from something else, by looking for a foundation or a root, that we lose our Being and by ascribing some kind of being to ourselves become doubtful of ourselves.

While gNyis-med Avadhūtipa gives an ethical interpretation of Saraha's last lines, Karma Phrin-las-pa interprets them metaphysically and existentially, Saṃsāra and Nirvāṇa are alike in being performances of Mind-as-such and, therefore, alike enjoyable in their being put on as a performance. Then, in acting out his own part simultaneously on both levels, the Saṃsāric and the Nirvāṇic, the individual deepens his existential awareness, but does not concretize it and so plant the seed of further limiting, traumatic experiences which only perpetuate his dividedness against himself. The person who can accept both levels has the capacity not only to enjoy life but also the ability to respond to life's challenges positively, because he has regained the spontaneity of his creative potential.

Karmamudrā and Jñānamudrā in Art

As has been shown in a previous chapter, Karmamudrā is the name for a situation in which persons—men and women—encounter each other and form a close and intimate relationship by mutually rewarding activities. This formation of a bond between two partners comprises several phases such as looking at each other, smiling at each other, touching and embracing each other, and finally engaging in copulation. This graded procedure has given rise to a classification of Tantric literature, which like all classifications contains a certain evaluation and which very much indicates how the person who made the classification felt towards a given subject-matter. One such classification declares:

> "In the Golden Age, emotions were few and the partners were satisfied by looking at each other. Hence the Kriyātantras. . . . In the following age, there arose the desire to find satisfaction by smiling at each other. Hence the Caryātantras. . . . In the subsequent age, the partners became desirous of satisfaction by touching and embracing each other. Hence the Yogatantras. . . . In our degenerate age, the Anuttarayogatantras are for those desirous of sexual intercourse. . . ."[179]

Here we easily recognize the potent myth of a Golden Age, which sums up the feeling that somewhere, at some time, things must have been better—'the good old days' as contrasted with 'the decline of standards'. Essentially this myth brings into focus the discontent that irks us at this moment and makes us attribute the freedom from our particular discontent to a bygone age. But it is not merely discontent that irks us, there also is the feeling of insecurity, of fear and self-condemnation. We tend to reject a part of ourselves and, in the end, this rejection destroys an individual's dignity and incapacitates him from doing anything: I am angry at myself; I am afraid of and try to run away from myself; I feel guilty and ashamed, depending on the indoctrination I have received on the basis of socially approved standards of behaviour, varying from time to time and from one class of people to another. " 'In the good old days' people didn't do such things, so you shouldn't do them 'now'." But when the person who does 'such things' is then ostracized and made to feel guilty, he soon will become convinced not only that he is bad but that he lives in a 'degenerate' age because all do what he is made to feel bad about.

Self-condemnation is self-destructive, not self-constructive. It decreases the pleasure and joy of living and reduces life to boredom and dullness. There is, therefore, another classification which emphasizes a creative approval of life:

> "The Kriyātantras are for the dull; the Caryātantras for those of medium intelligence; the Yogatantras for those of superior and the Anuttarayogatantras for those of highest intellectual capabilities."[180]

Certainly, the dull are blinded by their traditional doctrines and taboos and there is little likelihood of spiritual growth and self-development. Only those who break away from traditional patterns have the chance of finding new ways of life. The emphasis on the deepening of one's understanding is at the same time a warning against the naive assumption that the popularity of an idea is its validity. More often than not, popularity depends on and is 'pushed' by the mass media pretending to enlighten people while actually keeping them dull and stupid.

The creative approach to life begins with a creative imagination which itself starts with an acceptance and appreciation of reality. Its aim is not to make reality conform to one's illusions but to understand it better so as to enrich one's experience of it. Karmamudrā is a real-life situation which through the Jñānamudrā is experienced more meaningfully, and more satisfactorily. As real life-situations, both Karmamudrā and Jñānamudrā present themselves as enthralling themes for the poet, the sculptor, the painter, and even the dancer.

Actually, in Indian conception, a knowledge of the dance is the first requirement for the pursuit of any other art. The dancer is 'enacting' life's drama, he 'presents' a sequence of image-units which in their combination reveal an immense variety of situations whose 'embodiment' is the dancer himself. The accent on rhythm and movement is recognizable in Indian sculpture as well. We have only to point to the sinuous curves of the thin waist and the swelling hips and breasts of the female nudes and semi-nudes; Indian sculpture invites us to share in the life of its figures, which is both an intuitive and an intellectual experience. Their beauty does not reside in isolation in an unattainable or charmed realm of abstract perfection, but in the concrete and whole content. Therefore, the Indians did not speak of beauty or aesthetic value, but of *rasa*, 'life-sap', comprising what we separate into sentiment, emotion, meanings, values; and therefore also Indian sculpture is 'presentation' rather than 're-presentation'. Representation presupposes another thing that is somehow made to reappear under the guise of an 'art-object'; presentation retains the vitality that belongs to the work of art in its own right. Being a presentation, the very presence of a work of art can open our eyes to the real world in such a way that we seem to see it for the first time in its pristine newness. The presence itself is something paradoxical, for it is both something and nothing. The something (*snang-ba*, *gzugs*) is attested by the fact that there is something *present*, the nothing (*stong-pa*) by the fact that this something is not a presence *of* any thing. sGam-po-pa speaks of this realization as the opening of the eyes of a blind man, and his first example is:[181]

> "All that appears in such a variety of appearance as earth, stone, rocks, mountains, grass, trees, forests, men and women and so on, is nothing as such in its appearance, because it is devoid of any essence (that would make appearance an entity in itself). It is the self-manifestation of this Being nothing in itself, in a variety of appearances.

In brief, appearance and the openness of Being are not a duality. So also is stated in the *Prajñāhṛdaya:*

> 'Form (*rūpa*) is (an) open (dimension); the open dimension (of Being, *śūnyatā*) is form. This open dimension is not different from form, and form is not different from the open dimension of Being.'

Furthermore, although a mirage appears as water, there has never been a drop of water in it, because it has no essence. In the same way appearance and openness of Being are not a duality, and one should not regard them as being so. In so regarding them there is no hankering after appearance, and when one experiences such a lack of hankering, one becomes free from feelings of joy over success and feelings of disappointment in the face of failure."

The aesthetic awareness remains supremely indifferent to what from the ordinary standpoint must appear to be life's 'real' concerns. It makes men live in the free possibilities of being, where *nothing has* to be, but *everything can* be. In the field of art one must not confuse artistic with philosophical theorizing. The awareness of the open dimension of Being was continuously and sufficiently present to influence the imagination of the artist and of the Buddhist philosophers, since the aesthetic and spontaneous are prior to the practical and the intellectual. The significance of the openness of Being for the human body, both in its earthly life and its presentation in art is revealed in sGam-po-pa's short statement:

> "Through freedom from the defects of appearance the limits of Saṃsāra are abolished and this (unity of) appearance and openness of Being is Nirmāṇakāya."[182]

The limits and, by implication, the limitations of Saṃsāra are our tendency to reduce and, by a progressive partiality and biasedness, to become blind to the full life. The Nirmāṇakāya, on the other hand, as sensuous embodiment contains within it something revelatory of this full life. Nirmāṇakāya is an 'expression', not a description; through it Being is manifested. And since all art is primarily concerned with Being rather than with finite and transitory re-presentations, the artist creating a work of art does not merely exteriorize his feelings and emotions but explores them in a new setting that can stand in place of the one that threatens his very Being and in which he can live in a better and more satisfying way.

Karmamudrā is the familiar setting of men and women meeting and becoming intimate with each other, and, as Nāropa pointed out in his description of the Karmamudrā situation, persons here tend to focus on some particular item and to derive from that starting point similarly demarcated items as acceptable for and conducive to a certain purpose. The artist, however, does not start with such well-defined items, but makes visually present and vividly concrete an apprehended prospect revealing values to be realized in life—the first meeting of (prospective) lovers, the consummation of their love, and all that lies between and comes afterwards. In this respect all art projects an implicit view of life or being, which also plays a central role in determining the kind of art we will respond to, because it is in the works of art that man's basic values, not necessarily his professed values, but the actual values of being, are expressed.[183] Thus, the pleasure a person takes in his being, seeing life as a value and feeling himself to constitute a value, as well as the pleasure he takes in another person's being by admiring his or her existence as a value, fuse in the feeling of love whose celebration, in the realm of Karmamudrā, is sex as the concrete experience of the joy and value of life. The rich suggestiveness and the implicit interaction of value and action—it is in the nature of a value that action is required to realize and to maintain it; and it is in the nature of action to strive for and to enact values—is most clearly brought out in the sculptures of Nāgārjunakoṇḍa[184] (Plates I-IX), all of which reveal a sensuous and spontaneous joy, expressive of an intense love of life. The female figures have been rendered with loving care and their lithe grace invites the beholder to follow each of their contours displaying both elegance and seductiveness, while the male figures express vigour and self-confidence. Each figure is a wordless presentation of what life feels like, of how it feels to be pleasurably excited. That such 'erotic' sculptures are found on temples is most opportune, because thereby a view of life as exultation and celebration is manifested. They have, of course, no place in a view of life as tragic doom, where self-confidence is replaced by self-loathing and where the abiding and central theme is death.

While the Karmamudrā emphasizes vitality, it is through her interpretation in art—art is always interpretation and anticipated meaning, never a copy or duplication—that she imperceptibly fuses with the Jñānamudrā as the actual instrument of insight (Plates X-XIV). Through the Jñānamudrā living forms are presented to our imagination which, unlike discursive reasoning, is creative. Not only does it lift our sensibility out of the stress of ordinary life into a condition of serenity, it also makes us increasingly aware of new intimations of reality. Wherever art takes a motif from the 'actual' world, be this a human figure, a flower, any theme from life, it transforms it into an image of the imagination and imbues it with vital meaning. Through creative imagination our ordinary reality becomes 'significant', but its significance cannot be demonstrated, as this or that ingredient that has gone into the making of a sculpture or a painting or a poem can be pointed out. We apprehend it by insight and are confronted by it. Confrontation means to come face-to-face with reality. Hence, in artistic rendering, the frontal aspect dominates. The images are to be looked at from the front only, and they hold the beholder's gaze unswervingly captive so as to let him find ever deeper meanings and to prevent him from relapsing into the world of deadening opinions. As a result feeling and image are so perfectly and completely resolved into one another that absolute lucidity of meaning is present.

Works of art tell us about the import that Being has for man by expressing and clarifying deep-rooted emotions. Consequently man's place in the world is made a little more transparent than it has been before. What the sculptor or painter does wordlessly, the poet achieves by his diction. Each one, in his own way, iconizes Being which he discerns through the familiar events of daily life as having pertinence to him. For the common occurrences of everyday life are themselves avenues through which

Being is manifested, and as such they are open to all. Only in this sense can we relate the various arts to each other. Thus Plate I seems to make visible Bhāravi's words:

> "Knowing that the blue lotus at the young woman's ear, in colour like her eyes, is of no avail alone, Intoxication, like a friend, added lustre by loving glances."[185]

Plates V and VI, Māgha's verses:

> "As if it had been properly propitiated, all of a sudden Wine granted them a boon: it dispelled the frigidity of shyness and led the lovers to the bliss of love's consummation."[186]

and:

> "Embarrassed by the removal of her blouse, and as if to block the path of his gaze, one woman covered her breasts with her husband's broad chest."[187]

Plates II *a* and *b* illustrate Bhāravi's verses:

> "Put aside your anger, go to your lover, or your fickle heart will soon be sad." Thus a clever friend beseeched a girl wanting to go to her lover.[188]

and:

> "O you lovely girl, who resemble a young creeper, do not fatigue yourself by waving your hands! Why should the swarm of bees have come under the impression that you were the wish-granting creeper. Fly from here."[189]

Plates IV and VII remind us of Amaru's words:

> " 'I have a word for you', he said and drew me to a lonely spot; and since my heart was eager I sat close to him. Then whispering into my ear and sniffing my face he caught hold of my braid of hair and drank the nectar of my lips."[190]

and:

> "When the house-parrot, having overheard the words the married couple had exchanged during the night, repeated them too frankly in the presence of their elders, the young wife, overcome by shame, stuck a small ruby from her ear-ornament into the parrot's beak as if to give it a pomegranate seed in order to stop its talking."[191]

Plate IX reflects what Rādhā told her lover Kṛṣṇa after their love-play:

> "Arrange my tresses that roused your amorous play, round my temples purer than the lotus-flower."[192]

Insight into life and Being ultimately springs from creative, and by implication, artistic imagination. Therefore the fine arts not only can give us knowledge, but also, through their influence on our lives, give form to our emotive experiences. The close relationship between Tantrism and the fine arts underlines the importance of learning to see reality as a symbol of life and feeling, not as a sign that points to something other than itself. The meaning of life is in living it.

Notes

1 p. 153.
2 Nāro, fol. 5b. This work is a commentary on the *Āhapramāṇa-samyak-nāma-ḍākinī-upadeśa*, a survey of Tantric ideas and practices.
3 ibid., folls. 6b-7a. The levels mentioned here include the preparatory stage, the accumulation of knowledge and merits, leading to the ten spiritual levels discussed in the Sūtras, in addition to which three higher levels are recognized in Tantrism, the highest one being the level of a Sceptre-holder. Further details are found in *bSre-'pho*, foll. s9b f.
4 ibid., fol. 7a.
5 ibid.
6 ibid.
7 II 2, 35f.
8 Nāro, fol. 7b.
9 'Three manifestations' (*snang-ba gsum*) is a symbolical term for intra-psychic processes. The 'dimming of the radiant light' (*snang*) refers to the first movement towards the developing split into subject and object; the 'diffused glow' (*mched*) indicates the growing dependence upon the object; and the 'settled gloom' (*thob*) marks the state of the final loss of intrinsic awareness. This symbolism takes on different meanings in different contexts. See H. V. Guenther, *The Life and Teaching of Nāropa*, pp. 274f., sGam-po-pa, Ki 10b.
10 Nāro, fol. 10b.
11 sGam-po-pa, Tsa 3b.
12 Nya 53b.
13 Dharmakāya (*chos-sku*) is a term for the experience of Being in one's own existence (*sku*) in the sense that Being is an absolute reality and value (*chos*). The experience is 'ineffable' in the sense that any attempt to conceptualize it would detract from its validity of absoluteness by reducing it to some content in mind which is relative to other contents. 'Ineffable' therefore does not mean that 'ineffability' is a quality of Dharmakāya. The experience of Being operates through Sambhogakāya (*longs-sku*) and Nirmāṇakāya (*sprul-sku*), both of them referred to by the term Rūpakāya (*gzugs-sku*). Sambhogakāya and Nirmāṇakāya are thus images through which we understand our existential value of Being. In particular, Sambhogakāya is an empathetic experience through which we take empathetic delight in Dharmakāya or Being. Nirmāṇakāya 'expresses' this experience in such a way as to communicate it to others. Dharmakāya is also used as a term for Being-as-such in which all that is participates and by

XV. Maṇḍala of Avalokiteśvara, Tantric form (*Author's collection*)

XVI. Maṇḍala of Mañjuśrī (*Author's collection*)

virtue of it *is*. sGam-po-pa, Ca 20b f. says: "The whole of the phenomenal universe has never come into existence (as something other than and apart from Being-as-such) and is of the nature of Dharmakāya. Pure from its very beginning and beyond the limitations of propositional statements is what is meant by 'ineffability'. Stupid adepts who have no knowledge and no understanding seek Dharmakāya or the ineffable beyond or behind the phenomenal world which they negate and dismiss. They never find Dharmakāya despite their efforts. What they do is like attempting to find water beyond and behind ice. The defect of such ignorance is that by not knowing what the phenomenal world is (*yin-lugs*) one is unable to understand the presence of Being (*gnas-lugs*).'

14 'Level of formlessness', *ārūpyadhātu*, is an undifferentiated continuum from which 'aesthetic forms' (*rūpa*) emerge.

15 Nāro, fol. 12b f.

16 The idea of mind being a *tabula rasa* (blank tablet, a translation of the Greek *pinax agraphos*) has played a considerable role in Western thought. This idea is first found with Aeschylus, and continues through Plato, Aristotle, the Stoics, Thomas of Aquinas, to John Locke who gave prominence to it in his *Essays concerning human understanding* (II 1, 2) and who uses the term 'white paper' (from the Greek phrase *charten euergon eis apographein*). The Greek term is first used by Alexander of Aphrodisias (*ca.* −200), its Latin translation by Aegidius Romanus (died +1316). Locke's idea was criticized by Leibniz (*Nouveaux essais* I 1, 3; II 1 etc.) who clearly saw the fallacy of this idea which is self-destructive and self-negating.

17 The structure and energy dynamics of the human organism are referred to by the technical term *rtsa*, 'pathways' along which the life force moves. The indigenous texts clearly distinguish between the 'pathways' (*rtsa*), the 'movement of the life force' (*rlung*), and the 'life force' itself (*thig-le*). To speak of 'Tantric physiology' in this context is a superb example of what A. N. Whitehead has called 'misplaced concreteness'.

18 This bodily activity is technically known as *rlung* 'motility'. Motility is spontaneous movement. It does not imply displacement of something in space. Motility is the expression of the total living process. On the dynamics of structure and motility see sGam-po-pa, Khi 21b f.

19 *Nāro*, fol. 51b.

20 ibid., 58b.

21 ibid., 60b.

22 sGam-po-pa, Nga 11a and throughout his works.

23 *Toward a Psychology of Being, passim.*

24 *Zab-mo nang-don*, fol. 7b.

25 *Zab-mo nang-don rnam-'grel*, fol. 72a.

26 *bSre-'pho*, fol. 57a ff.

27 ibid.

28 sGam-po-pa, Tha 46b.

29 sGam-po-pa, Ca 20a.

30 sGam-po-pa, Nga 8a.

31 sGam-po-pa, Nga 11ab.

32 See above, p. 17.

33 'Unborn' refers to a central idea in Buddhism. Basic to it is an absolute reality principle which implies that reality or Being is one and that there can be no other being or reality without contradicting the initial premise. Since the fictions of the mind are but the working of absolute reality or Mind-as-such they are not something apart from it and in this sense are 'unborn'. If one assigns them a reality other than the absolute reality of Being they are seen to 'appear' and to 'disappear', to 'be born' and 'to 'die' and they engender the relativization of absoluteness through the contrast with the relativity of what there is or 'appears'.

34 This term corresponds to our 'over-evaluated idea'. See H. V. Guenther, *The Royal Song of Saraha*, pp. 83 ff.

35 See above, note 9.

36 sGam-po-pa, Cha 14a; Ha 3a; Ki 22b.

37 Mahāmudrā refers to the absoluteness of Being as it 'impresses' itself on us when we encounter our Being.

38 sGam-po-pa, Ca 26a f.

39 They are the five emotions which, being distortions of original awareness and bliss supreme, contain within them the possibility of recapturing this original awareness and bliss supreme. See below, pp. 54ff.

40 sGam-po-pa, Ca 27ab.

41 sGam-po-pa, Ta 4a: "Unknowing and togetherness-awareness (i.e., the spontaneity of the cognitive process) are like the palm and the back of one's hand. As long as one does not understand, (absolute Awareness or Mind-as-such) is said to be the root of Saṃsāra; when one understands, it is said to be the root of original awareness."

42 *bSre-'pho'i khrid*, fol. 67b.

43 sGam-po-pa, Ra 11ab.

44 The technical term *śūnya*(*tā*) indicates the 'open dimension of Being'. The customary translation by 'void' or 'emptiness' fails to convey the positive content of the Buddhist idea. This open dimension is 'nothing as such' in the sense that it cannot be reduced to a content of mind, and when the determinate contents of mind are of primary concern the openness of Being is readily dismissed as something nihilistic. The positive content may be gleaned from two verses by Saraha and his commentary on them:

> "*nga* stands for freshness, nothing in itself;
> If a yogi can continuously please
> The youthful mistress, without (indulging in ideas of) good and evil,
> The darkness of night will be annihilated and the radiant light unclosed."
>
> *Ka-khasya Doha*, fol. 55b
>
> "*na* stands for freshness, nothing in itself;
> When the fresh mind is understood (in its freshness),
> it is not sullied by good or evil
> And the youthful mistress is filled with spontaneity.
> Attending constantly (on her the yogi) is not subject to birth
> or death and is not fettered (in Saṃsāra)".
>
> *Ka-khasya Doha*, fol. 56a

"*Ṇa* stands for *ṇaya* (*naya*) 'fresh'. Through a self-validating awareness freshness of mind is understood as an openness, but not as an intellectually induced emptiness. *Ṇa* stands for *ṇirantara* 'continuously'. When the yogi can continuously abide in spontaneity, (he enjoys) bliss, because concepts and their verbalizations have stopped. At that time—*ṇa* stands for *ṇa-si* (*nāśa* 'destruction') 'night'. Darkness of night means frustration by infatuation. Since 'appearance' as it comes to ordinary persons, is not present, there is nihilism, frustration. When this appearance of frustration has stopped there comes 'appearance' as it is for the yogi, the radiant light as an utter openness".

Ṭippaṇa, fol. 58b.

"*Ṇa* stands for *ṇaya* (*naya*) or *ṇi-dza* (*nija*) 'the fresh mind'. The fresh mind has never been set up by causes and conditions; it is genuine, conceptless, a radiant light. Such a mind is nothing in itself; this means that it is not something that has been emptied. *Ṇa* stands for *ṇiyamana* (*nijamanas*) 'fresh mind'. When freshness is understood, there is nothing of good or evil present. Since there are no concepts, (this freshness) is not sullied. *Ṇa* stands for *ṇayaghari* (*nayagharinī*) 'youthful mistress'. 'She is filled with spontaneity' means that she is happy; she is not glad or happy by way of concepts. *Ṇa* also stands for 'spontaneity' and for *ṇi-ba-ra* (?) 'continuously'. When one continuously stays with her, one is not subject to birth, old age and death. The meaning is that only Saṃsāra is bondage".

Ṭippaṇa, fol. 60b.

The feminine symbolism shows that mind is the matrix of ideas and that its (her) function is to inspire.

45 sGam-po-pa, Cha 2b.

46 sGam-po-pa, Tha 20ab.

47 sGam-po-pa, Nya 5a-6a.

48 MN I 169ff.

49 *Jñānasiddhi* VII 3.

50 *Mahāsukhaprakāśa* 6.

51 *Prajñopāyaviniścayasiddhi* I 27.

52 *Dohā* no. 27.

53 Unless otherwise stated the quotations are from Saraha's Dohākoṣa, in Tibet popularly known as 'People Dohās'. There exists a fragmentary Apabhraṃśa version which has been translated into French by M. Shahidullah, *Les Chants Mystiques de Kāṇha et de Saraha*. See H. V. Guenther, *The Royal Song of Saraha*, pp. 8 ff.

54 *Ṭīkā*, fol. 101ab.

55 The term 'true Guru' (*bla-ma dam-pa*) is one of the many symbolical expressions used in Tantric works. It refers to the absoluteness of Being, not to a person, as it 'impresses' itself on the individual coming closer to his being. In a certain sense the 'true Guru' can be compared with our idea of 'conscience' though not in its traditional meaning of 'negative voice', but rather in the positive interpretation suggested by Rollo May, as man's capacity to tap his deeper levels of insight and to be more aware and appreciative of reality. See Rollo May, *Man's Search for Himself*, p. 184. Although guidance seems to come

from 'within' and a higher value has 'taken over', this does not imply passivity or passivism on the part of the individual. As the simile implies, a self-expanding awareness is at work and makes the individual more sensitive and appreciative and hence more active in a meaningful way, in contrast with the compulsive activism of the person whose only qualification is that he knows and understands nothing.

56 'Memory' (*dran-pa*) is a technical term summing up the conscious processes. See H. V. Guenther, *The Royal Song of Saraha*, passim.

57 *Doha skor-gsum*, fol. 52b. The identity of Bliss and absolute Being is also affirmed by sGam-po-pa, Nga 12a.

58 Karma Phrin-las-pa in his *Doha skor-gsum*, fol. 35a, explicitly states that concepts belong to the mind of an ordinary person, bliss to Buddhahood. The Tibetan term *'gro-ba* contains a pun as it means both 'sentient being' and 'moving about'.

59 'Sacrifice' means the surrender of a higher value in favour of a lower value or no value. To sacrifice life is to espouse death, a no-value. The surrender of a lower value in favour of a higher one is 'gain'.

60 *Nāro*, fol. 21a.

61 ibid.

62 ibid.

63 *yid* (*manas*) is distinguished from *sems* (*citta*) which refers to the intentionality of mind, by emphasizing the subjective disposition.

64 gNyug II 41ab. Similarly sGam-po-pa, Ra 10a, says: "While the evil of conceptualization arises in a mind (*sems*), Mind-as-such (*sems-nyid*) stays unborn. Its unbornness is its ceaseless dynamics. Because of these ceaseless dynamics of unbornness, understanding leads to Buddhahood, non-understanding into Saṃsāra. By way of analogy, mustard seed has an oily fertility, if one plants the seed it grows into a plant, if one presses it it yields oil. Because of the ceaseless dynamics of unbornness, these dynamics in manifesting themselves as intrinsic perception become Dharmakāya; in manifesting themselves as unknowing they become a sentient being. These dynamics rise as unknowing and alienation as long as one is a sentient being; they rise as understanding and experiencing when one is a yogi travelling the Path; and they rise as value-being (Dharmakāya) and original awareness when one has become a Buddha."

65 See above, note 13.

66 This term is used for the more 'theoretical' aspect of Buddhism as discussed in the philosophical schools. See H. V. Guenther, *Treasures on the Tibetan Middle Way*, p. 52.

67 This term refers to the more 'practical' application of the 'theoretical' discussions. See H. V. Guenther, *Treasures on the Tibetan Middle Way*, p. 53.

68 SN II 179.

69 AN II 211.

70 AN II 10.

71 AN II 34.

72 *Visuddhimagga*, p. 567.

73 ibid., p. 568.

74 *Prasannapadā*, p. 530.

75 For further details see H. V. Guenther, *Buddhist Philosophy in Theory and Practice*.
76 Quoted in *Advayavajrasaṃgraha*, p. 2.
77 *Mahāsukhaprakāśa*, 13.
78 *bSre-'pho*, fol. 69b.
79 The image itself is already found in Saraha's *Kāyakośāmṛtavajragīti*. Saraha uses it to illustrate the growth of bliss:

> "First appearance is experienced as being open,
> This is like knowing ice to be water.
> Then, while the appearance of 'memory' does not stop,
> Its openness becomes indistinguishable from bliss,
> This is the stage when ice turns into water.
> When 'memory' dissolves into 'non-memory', and this into 'unorigination' and
> Everything has turned indistinguishably into bliss supreme,
> This is like ice having turned into water." (fol. 112a.).

80 *Lam-zab*, fol. 24b.
81 *Mahāyānasūtrālankāra* IX 67-68.
82 *Jñānasiddhi* I 48-49.
83 sGam-po-pa, Ca 32a.
84 *Nāro*, fol. 61a.
85 ibid.
86 The Prāsangikas at first challenged the various philosophical systems by pointing out their inherent inconsistencies, but did not set up a system of their own. Later on they developed a system of their own. See H. V. Guenther's *Buddhist Philosophy in Theory and Practice*, pp. 141 ff. Reference here is made to the negative interpretation of the 'openness of Being' (*śūnyatā*) as 'absolute negation' (*med-dgag, prasajyapratiṣedha*).
87 *Nāro*, fol. 61b.
88 See also above note 17.
89 They are then termed *'khor-lo* (*cakra*). These focal points become intelligible when viewed from the energy dynamics of the human body, but not by attempting to identify them with parts of the organism.
90 *Doha skor-gsum*, fol. 21a.
91 See H. V. Guenther, *The Life and Teaching of Nāropa*, pp. 143 ff. Although the empowerments are placed here in an 'objective' context, there is a considerable symbolism involved.
92 That is, to conceive of the body as a god, of speech as mantra, and of mind as absolute Being. See also below, p. 63.
93 Reference here is to polar drives and feelings which have their basis in the unity and antithesis of living processes. The polar forces indicated here correspond to what in our terminology now is love and sex. As is well known, in sex the feeling of vitality flows downwards, charging the pelvic region and the genital organs; in love this feeling flows upwards, expanding the horizon of meaning and encompassing the love object which becomes the whole of the lover's world. The downward flow from the head end (brain) to the tail end (the genital organs) is termed *Yas-babs* (also *yas-brtan*) 'descent from

above', and the upward flow *mas-brtan* 'steadying from below'. Although the feelings moving downwards have a different *quality* from those moving upwards, they are *quantitatively* alike. Both ends are equal in their capacity to hold and focus the energy whose movement is pendular in nature. Sexual feeling is directly proportionate to the feeling of love and vice versa. Thus the *potential* of sex, unless undermined by an artificially induced sense of guilt and conflict, offers the individual the most intense and unique form of experiencing his Being, which always occurs in pleasure and joy, never in a feeling of life's futility or of the individual's servitude to an incomprehensible postulate. The potential of sex can offer this chance because it belongs to the total individual, not to one of his many aspects alone. In certain texts, *Sekoddeśaṭīkā*, p. 25, for instance, it is stated that in the union between man and woman 'the *bodhicitta* must not be discharged'. The use of the term *bodhicitta*, rich in symbolical content, is ample evidence that it is not primarily a matter of avoiding an ejaculation. It rather serves as an advice not to allow the pulsatory movement that unites the different aspects of man's personality (i.e., love and sex) to be disrupted. Moreover, the conscious attempt at preventing an ejaculation introduces conceptual (inhibitory) operations which in this specific case are known to result in erective impotence and which are characteristic of the schizoid person and his obsession with sex as a means of establishing contact with others (see Alexander Lowen, *Physical Dynamics of Character Structure*, *The Betrayal of the Body; Pleasure*). When in *Prajñopāyaviniścayasiddhi* V 40 it is stated: "But he must proceed in such a way that the mind (*manas*) is not agitated", the use of the word *manas* emphasizes the fact that love must not be dissociated from sex nor sex from love. The *manas* is the function that sets up the sense of ego-centredness and then acts as categorical perception. Through it sex and love become opposing categories.

94 *blo-las 'das-pa*: 'going beyond the (confines of the) intellect', not beyond Mind-as-such or Being-as-such.

95 *Ṭīkā*, 71b.

96 *Nāro*, fol. 81a.

97 We have only to remind ourselves of the venomous outpourings of a St. Jerome, a St. Odo of Cluny and others, and of the Church-fanned witch-hunt epidemics; after all, if the queen of heaven is a perpetual virgin, the ordinary terrestrial woman is an abomination and can (or must?) be saved from going to perdition by further humiliation and punishment. The statements against woman, found in some Buddhist scriptures, are on a quite different level as they are not part and parcel of the doctrinal system. No woman has ever been tortured or killed 'in the name of The Buddha', but the number of those 'in the name of God' is countless.

98 Kāṇha, *Dohā* no. 29.

99 *Nāro*, fol. 77a. cp. 81a.

100 ibid., fol. 82a.

101 *Vyaktabhāvānugatatattvasiddhi*.

102 *Sekoddeśaṭīkā*, p. 56.

103 *Nāro*, fol. 87a. See also above, note 93.

104 *Doha skor-gsum*, fol. 22ab.

105 These are symbols for polarities otherwise termed Saṃsāra and Nirvāṇa, the world of appearance and the open dimension of Being, and so on.

106 This numbering is taken from the mentalistic Yogācāra system which recognizes the common five sensory perceptions, categorical perception as the sixth perception, all of which stand in an asymmetrical relation to a centre providing the sense of ego, numbered the seventh perceptual event, which emerges out of a pervasive substratum capable of retaining traces of experience and their modifications, termed the eighth kind of awareness. See H. V. Guenther, *Buddhist Philosophy in Theory and Practice*, pp. 95 ff. for further details.

107 This term (*chags-lam*) refers to the situation in which sex and love are of major importance for the development of the individual.

108 The texts usually mention four mudras which are related to each other in the following way:

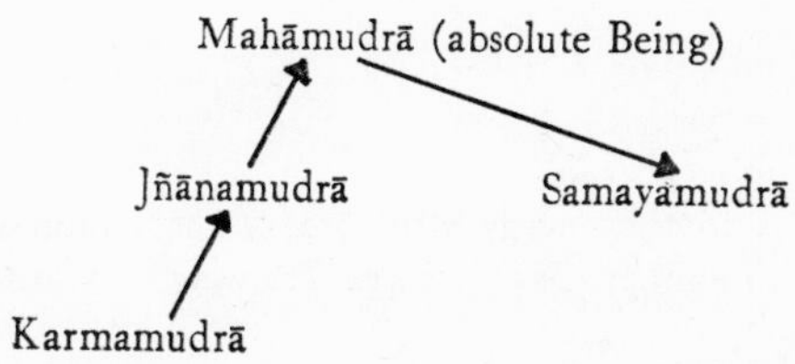

109 *Nāro*, fol. 86b.

110 *Sekoddeśaṭīkā*, p. 56.

111 Great Mother is a term for *prajñāpāramitā*, 'appreciative-discriminative awareness at its peak'.

112 *Nāro*, fol. 87a.

113 *maṇḍala* is used here in its common designation as an orientational centre embellished by its surroundings.

114 *Ṭīkā*, fol. 72b. *Doha skor-gsum*, fol. 67ab.

115 See *Doha skor-gsum*, fol. 69a.

116 See above, note 108.

117 *Nāro*, fol. 87b f.

118 *Doha skor-gsum*, fol. 59a: "Since the unity of Being, bliss supreme, is Lord of Saṃsāra and Nirvāṇa, we speak (of him who has realized it as) Master".

119 *Sekoddeśaṭīkā*, p. 25. See also above, note 93.

120 ibid., p. 3.

121 *Prajñopāyaviniścayasiddhi* V 22-23.

122 The term 'shape of woman' also contains a suggestion of the idea of polarity in the structure dynamics of the body. Since it is due to the body that there is a world for it, 'internal processes' are as much 'external stimulations'.

123 *Prajñopāyaviniścayasiddhi*, V 3-6.

124 ibid., V 38-39.

125 *Advayavajrasaṃgraha*, p. 23.

126 *Ṭīkā*, fol. 87b. Cp. *Doha skor-gsum*, 38a.

127 For further details see H. V. Guenther, *The Royal Song of Saraha*, p. 149.

128 *Dohā* no. 32. The same image is used in *Ṭīkā* fol. 95ab.

129 *Dohakośa-upadeśagīti* (*mi-zad-pa'i gter-mdzod man-ngag-gi glu*), popularly known as Queen Dohā.
130 *Doha skor-gsum*, fol. 59ab.
131 ibid., fol. 59b-60a.
132 ibid., fol. 60ab.
133 ibid., fol. 60b.
134 ibid.
135 ibid., foll. 60b-61a.
136 The Prāsangikas are meant here. See above, note 86.
137 *Doha skor-gsum*, fol. 61ab.
138 ibid., fol. 72ab.
139 Quotation from Saraha's *Dohakośa*.
140 *Doha skor-gsum*, fol. 73a.
141 *Dohakośa*.
142 Queen Dohā.
143 *Doha skor-gsum*, fol. 73ab.
144 Queen Dohā.
145 *Doha skor-gsum*, fol. 73b-74a.
146 Reference here is to the energy structure of the living organism. Further details in H. V. Guenther, *The Life and Teaching of Nāropa*, pp. 273 ff.
147 *Nāro*, fol. 7b.
148 ibid.
149 See above.
150 *Ṭīkā*, fol. 73ab.
151 *Advayavajrasaṃgraha*, p. 23.
152 *Sekoddeśaṭīkā*, p. 56.
153 ibid., p. 57.
154 *Advayavajrasaṃgraha*, p. 49.
155 ibid., p. 24.
156 ibid., p. 50.
157 *Ṭīkā*, fol. 73b-74a.
158 ibid., 74ab.
159 ibid., 74b.
160 ibid., 74b-75a.
161 *Doha skor-gsum*, fol. 25b.
162 *Ṭīkā*, 75a.
163 ibid., 77b.
164 *Nāro*, fol. 65b.
165 ibid., foll. 65b-66a.
166 The conventional and absolute truths. The unity of the two truths derives from the Yogācāra system where it is foreshadowed.
167 p. 149.
168 *Ṭīkā*, 101ab.
169 *Doha skor-gsum*, fol. 55b.
170 *Ṭīkā*, foll. 104b-105a.
171 *Doha skor-gsum*, fol. 59a.
172 ibid., fol. 56b.

173 The Svābhāvikakāya 'Being-as-such' is essentially a term of Buddhist metaphysics, while Mahāsukhakāya 'Being felt as bliss supreme' refers to the experience of Being-as-such.
174 *Ṭīkā*, fol. 105a.
175 ibid., fol. 105b.
176 ibid., fol. 75b-77a.
177 *The Mind and its Place in Nature.*
178 *Doha skor-gsum*, fol. 26a-27b.
179 *sNgags*, fol. 21b ff.
180 ibid.
181 Ca 36a
182 Ja 6b.
183 Art as a projection of 'how things might and could be' can provide us with invaluable emotional satisfaction. But the nature of this satisfaction again depends upon our deepest values and premises. If life is a value and if our premise is that we can be fully aware of life and live it out of this awareness, we will seek the pleasure of being alive and look for those values that enhance life. But if our 'value'-system is such that we desire that which leads to our (and others') destruction, we will inevitably wallow in projections of horror and human degradation. The violence and brutality so often depicted in Western art is the direct outcome of the West's metaphysical negativism.
184 The sculptures of Nāgārjunakoṇḍa belong to the third century. On the history and significance of Nāgārjunakoṇḍa see The History and Culture of the Indian People, volume II, The Age of Imperial Unity, 4th ed., Bombay 1968, pp. 224 ff.; 524 ff.
185 *Kirātārjunēya* IX 61.
186 *Śiśupālavadha* X 22.
187 ibid., X 42.
188 *Kirātārjuniya* VIII 8
189 ibid., VIII 7.
190 *Amaruśataka*, 66.
191 ibid., 65
192 *Gītagovinda* XII.

Bibliography

(Only primary sources listed)

A. Texts in Sanskrit and Pali:

Advayavajrasaṃgraha	(=*Gaekwad's Oriental Series No. XL.*)
Amaruśataka	(=*Poona Oriental Series No. 101. Poona 1959*)
Hevajratantra	(=*London Oriental Series, Volume 6. The translation of passages from or ascribed to this text is my own.*)
Jñānasiddhi	(=*Gaekwad's Oriental Series No. XLIV.*)
Kāṇha	(=*M. Shahidullah, Les Chants Mystiques de Kāṇha et de Saraha. Paris 1928*)
Kirātārjuniya	(=*Haridās Sanskrit Granthmālā 105. Varanasi 1961*)
Mahāsukhaprakāśa	*in Advayavajrasaṃgraha*
Mahāyāna-Sūtrālaṅkāra	(=*Asaṅga: Mahāyāna-Sūtrālaṅkāra. Exposé de la Doctrine du Grand Véhicule selon le système Yogācāra, édité et traduit d'après un manuscrit rapporté du Népal par Sylvain Lévi. Tome I—texte. Paris 1907*)
Prajñopāyaviniścayasiddhi	(=*Gaekwad's Oriental Series No. XLIV.*)
Prasannapadā	(=*Mūlamadhyamakakārikās (Mādhyamikasūtrās) de Nāgārjuna avec la Prasannapadā Commentaire de Candrakīrti. Publié par Louis de la Vallée Poussin. Bibl. Buddhica IX, 1912*)
Sekoddeśaṭīkā	(=*Gaekwad's Oriental Series No. XC.*)
Śiśupālavadha	(=*Vidyābhavan Sanskrit Granthmālā 8. Varanasi 1961*)
Anguttara-nikāya	*Pali Text Society Edition*
Saṃyutta-nikāya	*Pali Text Society Edition*
Visuddhimagga	*Pali Text Society Edition*

B. Texts available only in their Tibetan translations:

Kakhasya doha (Ka-kha'i do-ha)	(*bsTan-'gyur, rgyud-'grel, vol. Tsi, foll. 66a-68b. Peking ed.*)

Kakhasya Doha-ṭippaṇa (Ka-kha'i do-ha'i bshad-pa bris-pa) — (*ibid., foll. 68b-78a*)

Kāyakoṣa-amṛtavajra-gītā (sKu'i mdzod 'chi-med rdo-rje'i glu) — (*ibid., foll. 78a-85a*)

Doha-koṣopadeśa-gīti (mi-zad-pa'i gter-mdzod man-ngag-gi glu "Queen Doha") — (*ibid., foll. 34a-39b*)

Doha-koṣa-hṛdaya-arthagītā-ṭīkā (Do-ha mdzod-kyi snying-po don-gi glu'i 'grel-pa) — (*ibid., foll. 97a-138a*)

Vyaktabhāvānugatatattvasiddhi (dngos-po gsal-ba'i rjes-su 'gro-ba'i de-kho-na-nyid grub-pa) — (*ibid., vol. Mi, foll. 66b-72b*)

C. Indigenous Tibetan Works:

Doha skor gsum — (*=Do-ha skor-gsum-gyi ṭika sems-kyi rnam-thar ston-pa'i me-long*)

sGam-po-pa — (*=The Collected Works o- sGam-po-pa. 38 volumes*)

Nāro — (*=Jo-bo Nāropa'i khyad-chos bsre-'pho'i gzhung-'grel rdo-rje-'chang-gi dgongs-pa gsal-bar byed-pa*)

sNgags — (*=sNgags-kyi spyi-don tzhangs-dbyangs 'brug-sgra*)

gNyug — (*=gNyug-sems 'od-gsal-gyi don-la dpyad-pa rdzogs-pa chen-po gzhi-lam-'bras-bu'i shan-'byed blo-gros snang-ba*)

bSre-'pho — (*=bSre-'pho'i lam skor-gyi thog-mar lam dbye-bsdu*)

bSre-'pho'i khrid — (*=Jo-bo Nāropa'i khyed-chos bsre-'pho'i khrid rdo-rje'i theg-par bgrod-p'ai shing-rta chen-po*)

Zab-mo nang-don — (*=Zab-mo nang-gi don*)

Zab-mo nang-don rnam-'grel — (*=Zab-mo nang-don-gyi rnam-bshad snying-po gsal-bar byed-pa'i nyin-byed 'od-kyi 'phreng-ba*)

Index

A. SUBJECTS

Absoluteness, 110, 124, 150 ns. 33 and 37
abstraction, 28, 34, 54
acceptance, 51, 105, 141
action, 3, 4, 10, 14, 52, 87, 95, 106 f., 134, 144
  appropriate, 98 f., 103
  compassionate, 127
  meaningful, 104
  motivated, 105
  reflex-, 48
activity, 102
  compulsive, 46
  cycle of, 47, 49 f.
  karmic, 39, 43
  mental, 13, 57, 104
  motor-, 113
  sexual, 97
aestheticism, 29, 93
Akaniṣṭha, 57
Akṣobhya, 103, 104, 105, 107, 108
alienation, 46, 53, 87, 115, 152 n. 64
Amitābha, 103, 104, 105, 107
Amoghasiddhi, 103, 104, 105, 107
annihilation, 49
Anuttarayogatantra, 140, 141
anxiety, 26, 27, 48, 68
apparition, 28, 76
appearance, 12, 14, 17, 20, 24 f., 28, 30, 33, 53, 62, 70, 103, 108, 113, 116 f., 126, 132, 134, 137, 142, f., 151 n. 44, 153 n. 79
  -as-such, 24
  self-, 112
  world of, 22, 28, 61 f., 110, 116
appreciation, 13, 16, 20, 34, 80, 95, 105, 107, 127, 141
  aesthetic, 16
appropriation, 43, 44
arrogance, 54, 55, 66, 118, 130, 136, 137
art, 60, 85, 106, 142 ff., 157 n. 183
asceticism, 7, 8, 65, 97
Ātman, 118
attachment, 41, 42, 54, 55, 94
attention, 32, 35, 106
attitude, 29, 50 f., 95 ff., 117
attraction, 41, 48, 49
aversion, 41, 42
avoidance, 49
awakening, xi, 13, 14, 15
awareness, 3, 18, 38, 40, 54 f., 57, 62, 76, 88, 101, 105 ff., 113, 123, 127, 132, 136 f., 150 n. 41, 155 n. 111
  absolute, 24, 31
  aesthetic, 31, 143
  appreciative, 98
  conceptless, 34
  discriminative-appreciative, 79
  existential, 17 f., 84, 104
  fundamental, 18
  intrinsic, 41 f., 46 f., 51 ff., 61, 91, 99, 148 n. 9
  moral, 31
  non-dual, 92
  original, 15 ff., 20, 41, 44 f., 105, 108, 110, 133, 150 n. 39
  pure, 12
  self-validating, 23, 26, 92, 94, 114
  spontaneous, 90 f.
  unitary, 93

Becoming, 43, 44, 53, 102
Being, xi, 3 ff., 12, 26, 33 f., 40, 51, 53, 56, 57, 62, 67, 75, 88 f., 93 f., 96 f., 99 ff., 113, 124, 127 f., 139, 143, 148 n. 13, 150 ns. 33 and 37, 151 n. 55
  absolute 11, 13, 23, 34, 36, 55, 62, 153 n. 92
  absoluteness of, 85
  -as-value, 37
  authentic, 71, 81
  distorted, 43
  embodied, 44
  embodying, 21
  immediacy of, 114

manifestation, 10, 19, 21, 27, 34, 71, 125, 148 n. 9
  deviate, 45 f.
mantra, 62, 153 n. 92
Mantrayāna, 61, 70
Mantrayoga, 61
masculinity, 16, 64
meaning, 51, 78, 96
  horizon of, 3, 83, 85
  symbolical, 78
meditation, 117, 122, 130, 134, 136 f.
memory, 39, 61, 70, 103 f., 113 ff., 121, 128, 133, 136, 152 n. 56, 153 n. 79
merit, 45, 148 n. 3
milieu, 15 f., 21
mind, 6, 8, 15 f., 18, 20 ff., 32 f., 37, 50, 59, 61 f., 69 f., 72, 82, 92 f., 100, 109, 113, 115, 117, 119, 122 f., 124, 128, 130, 132 ff., 137, 139, 149 n. 16, 152 n. 64, 153 n. 92
  constructs of, 10, 34
  contents of, 112
  ego-centred, 18 f.
  natural, 130 f., 137
  nature of, 14
  presence of, xi, 16
  subjective, 43, 103, 105
Mind-as-such, 17 f., 23 ff., 30 f., 50, 53, 57, 85, 89, 120, 123 f., 128, 132 f., 134 ff., 138, 152 n. 64, 154 n. 94
mirror, 54 f.
misery, 38, 87
mood, 44 f., 106
  aestheticistic, 84
moon-stone, 38 f., 121
morality, 32
motility, xi, 9. 13 f., 18 ff., 61, 69, f., 111, 113, 149 n. 18
motivation, 9, 18 f., 43 f.
movement, 69 f.
mudrā, 81, 109, 155 n. 108
mysticism, 124

Nairātmyā, 73, 96
name and form, 43 f.
nature, human, 51, 53 f.
negativism, 7, 50, 58, 157 n. 183
Nirmāṇakāya, 12, 45, 114, 143, 148 n. 13
Nirvāṇa, 38 ff., 98 ff., 103, 117, 119 ff., 129, 135, 138
non-duality, 25, 109
non-existence, 14, 20, 32, 110
non-memory, 39, 61, 103 f., 113 ff., 153 n. 79
nothing-as-such, 30, 32 ff., 142
nothingness, 8, 115, 137

Object, 9 f., 16 f., 20, 27, 29 ff., 33, 49, 52, 62 f., 68, 70, 82 ff., 93, 95, 100 ff., 105 ff., 112, 115, 122, 127, 129, 135, 148 n. 9.
objectivity, 13
obsession, 97, 153 n. 93
openness, 15 f., 19, 33, 35, 58, 62, 70, 81 f., 99, 108, 110, 113, 116, 130, 132, 134, ff., 152 n. 86
opinion, 12, 32 f., 47, 101 ff., 106, 120
opinionatedness, 126
orgy, 97
originality, 114
origination, dependent, 20
  chain of, 41, 43 f.

Padma, 74, 84
pain, 41, 46, 87
passivity, 152 n. 55
path, 102, 119, 135, 137
pathways, 149, n. 17
pattern, 60, 105, 111
  central, 20
  habitual, 50
  linguistic, 10
  traditional, 141
  verbal, 113
perception, 16 f., 27, 44, 56, 70, 80 f., 82 f., 106 ff., 113, 123, 127, 133
  abstractive, 9
  aesthetic, 16, 29, 37, 59 f., 84, 89, 92 ff.
  categorical, 9, 29, 43, 54, 91 ff., 133 ff., 137 f., 154 n. 93, 155 n. 106
  ego-centred, 23
  empathetic, 128
  intrinsic, 16, 53, 88, 90, 99, 111, 133
  ordinary, 18, 22 f., 80, 84, 89, 106
  pure, 34
  sensory, 155 n. 106
  two types of, 22

B. TECHNICAL TERMS

I. Sanskrit and Pali

II. *Tibetan*